GEORGETOWN

A Quick History

INCLUDING

THE GEORGETOWN LOOP

by Kenneth Jessen

J. V. Publications
2212 Flora Ct.
Loveland, Colorado 80537

© Copyright 1996 by Kenneth Jessen

All rights reserved, including those to reproduce this booklet, or parts thereof, in any form, without permission in writing from the publisher.

First Edition

3 4 5 6 7 8 9

Printed in the United States of America

Cataloging:

Jessen, Kenneth Christian
Georgetown - A Quick History

Bibliography
Includes Index
1. Colorado - History - Georgetown. I. Title

ISBN: 1-928656-01-3

cover drawing: The Maxwell House by Kenneth Jessen
book design: Kenneth Jessen
photographs, contemporary: Kenneth Jessen
film processing and printing: Steve Gregory, The Custom Darkroom

ACKNOWLEDGMENTS

Leland Feitz began this series of quick histories using his extensive knowledge of the Cripple Creek area. There are many errors in the source material on Georgetown, and to make this as accurate an account as possible, Ron Neely, Historic Georgetown Inc., provided valuable suggestions to the manuscript. Also contributing her knowledge was Christine Bradley, Clear Creek County archivist. One of the leading Georgetown experts, Liston Leyendecker, Professor of History, Colorado State University, made additional contributions to the accuracy of this work. Kathy Swan at the Denver Public Library, Western History Department, helped gather photographs. This also applies to the excellent staff at the Colorado Historical Society library. What makes this book easy to read is the professional editing done by Chris Skellett. A special thanks goes to Jim Skellett, First Light Publishing, for selecting me as the author of this project.

Kenneth Jessen, 1996

Other books and booklets by Kenneth Jessen:

Railroads of Northern Colorado
Thompson Valley Tales
Trolley Cars of Fort Collins (booklet)
Eccentric Colorado
Colorado Gunsmoke
Bizarre Colorado
The Wyoming/Colorado Railroad (booklet)
Estes Park - A Quick History

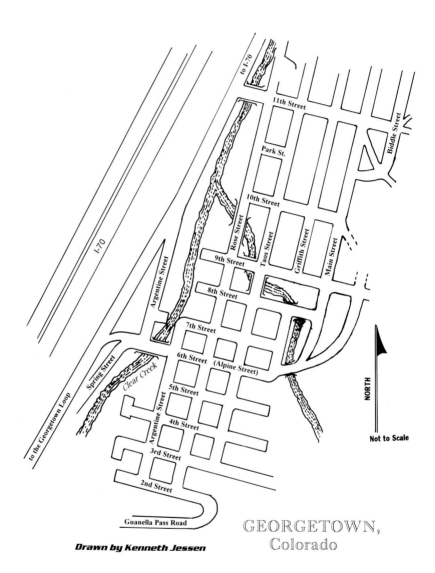

GEORGETOWN,
Colorado

Drawn by Kenneth Jessen

TABLE OF CONTENTS

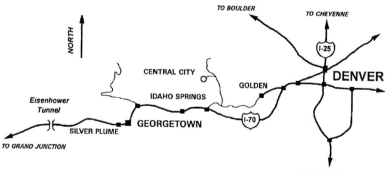

INTRODUCTION

A great deal of effort was made to provide not only historical photographs of Georgetown, but to also show the town the way it looks today. Many nineteenth century buildings remain standing, and the Hamill House and Hotel de Paris are open to the public.

Georgetown got started with the discovery of gold, but it would be silver which insured its three decades of prosperity. The demand for silver, however, was created artificially by the U.S. Government. When the purchase of silver began to deplete the gold reserves of the U.S. Treasury, the Sherman Silver Purchase Act was repealed. This happened in 1893, and the price of silver dropped to a point where most mines were uneconomical to operate. This ended the boom years for Georgetown. The demand for other metals during World War I would help slow Georgetown's decline, but eventually the majority of the town was abandoned. From a peak of about 5,000 residents, only a few hundred remained. It would be the post-war recreation era and tourism which would reverse Georgetown's decline.

The people who made Georgetown great included mining magnate William Hamill. He became one of Colorado's richest men, and over the years, transformed his simple home into the largest, most luxurious mansion in town. Another leading citizen was Jesse Summers Randall, founder and editor of *The Georgetown Courier*. He always sided with morality and decency. In contrast to Randall was mystery man Stephen Decatur who was editor of *The Colorado Miner*. He abandoned his first wife to fight in the Mexican War and abandoned his second wife to come to Colorado. Georgetown was also where Edward Wolcott got his start as a lawyer and went on to became a U.S. Senator. The Hotel de Paris was opened by Frenchman Louis Dupuy and became one of Colorado's leading hotels. Dupuy was born Adolphe Gerard, but after his desertion from the United States Army, he was forced to change his name.

No town was immune to violence. The town drunk, Edward Bainbridge, was hung by vigilantes for shooting James Martin at point blank range. Robert Schamle killed a German butcher just to steal money from his wallet. An angry Georgetown mob lynched Schamle over a hog pen. During a feud between two mining operations, Jackson Bishop gunned down mine owner and banker, Jacob Snider, in front the town's livery stable. Bishop made a clean getaway and was never tried for his crime.

The Pelican and Dives mines became locked in a legal dispute over ownership of a rich vein of silver ore common to both claims. Most of the battle took place in the court room, however some fighting erupted deep under ground and resulted in the death of two men. Over half a million dollars was spent in legal fees during the course of seven years.

Also closely linked to the town's history was the construction of the famous Georgetown Loop. To reach Silver Plume, the railroad used a complete spiral followed by two loops to reverse direction. This immediately became a tourist attraction, but after the decline of silver mining and the increased use of the automobile, mounting losses forced the railroad to abandon the Loop. In 1973, work began to restore the Georgetown Loop, and in 1984, the loop was completed to become a major area tourist attraction.

Hope you enjoy this short history of Georgetown.

Kenneth Jessen, Loveland, Colorado, 1996

It all began with the discovery by George and David Griffith of rich gold ore, but it would be silver which made Georgetown famous. This is the covered portal to the Capital Prize mine located near the original Griffith Mine at the east end of 11th Street at the top of a mine dump. (photograph by Kenneth Jessen)

New construction is very much in evidence in this early photograph of Georgetown looking north. On the left is a simple frame house which will be transformed into the Hamill House. (Colorado Historical Society F13769)

Taken prior to 1867, this early view of Georgetown is looking to the southeast with the smelter on the right spewing out smoke. A close examination of this photograph reveals no less than fifteen structures under construction. (Denver Public Library, Western History Department F140)

GEORGE'S TOWN

Rumors of gold in the Rocky Mountains swept across the prairie through Kansas Territory like a wild fire in 1858. William Green Russell and a small party of prospectors were able to pan a few hundred dollars in gold from a South Platte tributary. This modest discovery precipitated a gold rush where hundreds, then thousands of prospectors entered what was to become Colorado Territory.

Among the early arrivals were brothers George and David Griffith from Kentucky. They came to the new settlement of Auraria where Cherry Creek and the South Platte rivers joined. It was the fall of 1858, and the brothers constructed one of the first cabins in this fledgling town and settled down for the winter.

Believing that the early bird gets the worm, George A. Jackson and John H. Gregory made secret strikes during the early part of 1859. These were placer deposits located in the forks of Clear Creek. When the news got down to Auraria and Denver, anxious prospectors headed into the hills.

By the time the Griffith brothers arrived at what was to become Central City, the place was overrun, and in their estimation, all the good claims had been taken. The brothers moved on, and in June, 1859, they worked their way up the South Fork of Clear Creek past George Jackson's discovery, and traveled west to the end of a broad, unoccupied valley. They camped along the South Fork of Clear Creek, and here they discovered that panning yielded fifty cents to a dollar in gold flakes in every pan. Encouraged by their discovery, the brothers constructed a cabin at a location which would later become Georgetown. A couple of days later, George discovered the Griffith Lode on the side of what was later named Griffith Mountain. During the summer of 1859, the brothers recovered an estimated $500 in gold. Other prospectors arrived, and more claims were staked out. A camp began to form around the Griffith cabin, and it was christened George's Town.

David wrote the family back in Kentucky of the discovery. His two other brothers, John and William, their father along with John's wife, Elvira, made the long trip to Colorado and up Clear Creek to George's Town. It must have been a difficult trip, since only a primitive trail provided access to the area. Elvira was the first white woman to enter the valley.

To provide order and prevent claim jumping, the brothers formed the Griffith Mining District. Officers were appointed, and George became the recorder to register all mining claims. Gulch or placer claims were limited to one hundred feet in length in the gulch where a discovery was made, while lode claims were confined to one hundred feet by fifty feet in size. A 640-acre plat was laid out for George's Town, and it wasn't long before the name Georgetown was used.

This excellent winter photograph of Georgetown looking south shows Chimney Rock on the right and numerous cabins spread up on the sides of the mountains. A great deal of new construction is in evidence. (Colorado Historical Society F4961)

Getting mining equipment to Georgetown was next to impossible, so in 1860, the Griffiths took time away from mining and built a wagon road. It started near Central City at the head of Eureka Gulch and went over the mountains to Georgetown. It cost $1,500. It wasn't long before the

2

Griffiths used their new twenty mile long road to haul machinery for a stamp mill to crush their gold ore. The brothers charged a toll of $1 per round trip in an effort to recover their investment. They took in a little over $150 that first summer. The following spring, 1861, they added a toll gate. *The Rocky Mountain News* suggested that an assessment be made on all the mines in the Central City - Georgetown area to buy the road from the Griffiths. The road was purchased and opened to the public.

The mill built by the brothers was powered by water brought by a flume from Clear Creek. The diverted water fell over the top of a water wheel to power six stamps used to crush the gold-bearing rock. The mill began pounding rock into powder in 1861 and was the second mill to begin operations in Georgetown.

The Griffith mine was located high on the mountainside; an ore chute a thousand feet long was used to get the ore to the valley floor. The Griffith lode was mined through a twenty-five foot deep shaft.

Downstream from Georgetown, the Griffith brothers claimed part of the Clear Creek valley on behalf of their father, Jefferson Griffith. In 1861, they built a cabin for him, but unfortunately, he passed away the same year. The place became known as Mill City, and its name was later changed to Dumont.

By March 1861, Georgetown had forty residents, and the future looked bright. As summer approached, mining activity began to decline. The ore was becoming more difficult to mill as the depth of the mines increased. No longer was it possible to use primitive mechanical crushing methods followed by amalgamation with mercury. Near the surface, ore was naturally decomposed, but at depth, more sophisticated milling techniques were required. Much of the ore contained silver, but the milling process focused only on gold.

These mining difficulties were compounded by Elvira's fear of invasion by Indians. The Griffiths moved from the area in September, 1862, and in January of the following year, sold their property to Stephen Nuckolls. Nuckolls paid $10,000 for the Griffith property. In the fall of 1863, he rebuilt the mill, and it operated under the ownership of a company in New York.

What was to make Georgetown famous was the discovery on September 14, 1864 of silver ore high on McClellan Mountain to the south with ore values of over $800 per ton. After this discovery, Georgetown began to grow once again. Men with experience in processing the complex silver ore arrived, which insured success. The Argentine Mining District was established to handle the numerous silver claims. As for Georgetown, the crude cabins began to be replaced with more substantial structures made of milled lumber. Local saw mills were kept busy. By 1868, the town's population reached 1,500.

Taken sometime during the 1880s by William H. Jackson, this view is looking almost due north from the Green Lake Road. In the center of town is the three-story Cushman Block, Georgetown's tallest building. (Denver Public Library, Western History Department F38292)

4

On the left and in front of a mining company office is Jesse Summers Randall, founder and editor of The Georgetown Courier. *On the right is pioneer founder and editor of* The Rocky Mountain News, *William N. Byers. Ben Catren, Sr., local mine owner, is in the middle. This same structure stands today. (Denver Public Library, Western History Department F33031)*

This view of Georgetown, looking southeast, shows how densely packed the town was in the narrow Clear Creek Valley with stores lining 6th Street cutting across the photograph. The large, white, two-story structure on the right is the Clear Creek County Courthouse. Few of the structures in the foreground survive today. (Denver Public Library, Western History Department F659)

Looking southwest sometime after 1890, shows a town with buildings constructed primarily of milled lumber. The brick Cushman Block clearly visible as the large, dark-colored structure to the left of center. The road leading to Silver Plume can be seen cutting across the base of Republican Mountain. (Denver Public Library, Western History Department F38168)

This is how Georgetown looked after 1900 with the Julius Pohle House in the lower left hand corner along the road to Silver Plume. Chimney Rock to the right-center is void of its smokestack. (Denver Public Library, Western History Department Mc166)

6

THE SILVER QUEEN

Silver was discovered in the Georgetown area as early as 1860, but for the most part, this precious metal was ignored. Prospectors were intent on duplicating the success of rich gold deposits discovered by Jackson and Gregory. At the time, the U.S. Government placed silver coins at less than their metallic value on the open market, which meant the a great deal of silver currency was melted and sold. Even though the U.S. was on a bimetallic standard, gold dominated the currency.

High assay values in dollars per ton were placed on early silver lodes which changed the minds of the prospectors. In 1864, the Civil War caused high inflation in paper currency, and prices for precious metals reflected this fact.

Now that prospectors and mine owners were beginning to focus on silver, it would take several years before the ore could actually be converted into bullion. By 1865, prospectors were staking hundreds of claims in the Georgetown area. Such activity was usually accomplished by a group of individuals working together. Some would deed their claims for a dollar to one person. This allowed single owners to control many claims within an area to fend off any rivals for ore from the same vein.

In November, 1865, John Herrick mined high grade silver ore from the Adams and Hise lodes on Republican Mountain. The ore was packed down on the backs of burros to Black Hawk for smelting. Later, these mines were consolidated and became the Lebanon group.

To reduce the cost of transportation, Georgetown mine owners began to build their own mills. During 1866, three mills were under construction within the town. John Herrick supervised the construction of the Georgetown Smelting Works, powered by Clear Creek water.

In 1867, Caleb Stowell completed a furnace specifically designed for silver ore from a mine located high on McClellan Mountain to the south of Georgetown. Ore was put into sacks and transported by donkeys. The furnace failed to yield any silver, so Stowell turned to mill operator Frank Dibben. To make it more interesting, Dibben bet Stowell $500 that he could produce pure silver within 24 hours.

The wager was accepted and Dibben worked frantically behind closed doors using Stowell's mill. An hour before midnight, Dibben admitted defeat. He was replaced by black mill operator Lorenzo Bowman who knew how to treat this type of ore. Bowman had fifteen years of experience with galena-lead ore and smelter operation in Missouri. He was a member of a group of blacks who arrived in Clear Creek County in 1865.

Frank Dibben built this primitive smelter in 1868, and it was one of the first such plants in the Argentine District near Georgetown. The smelter was powered by a water wheel located on the opposite side. Dibben was noted for being the first mill operator to attempt to extract silver bullion from ore in Georgetown. (Denver Public Library, Western History Department F141)

Bowman had been secretly watching Dibben and his assistants through a knot hole in the wall of the mill and knew just what mistakes Dibben made. Bowman told Stowell that Dibben would certainly fail and asked for the opportunity to try his hand. Stowell granted Bowman permission, and by noon of the following day, Bowman was casting silver bullion simply by using more heat during the roasting process. This was a first silver bullion cast in Clear Creek County and marked a turning point in the history of the region. Now silver ore could be smelted in the immediate area saving on transportation costs.

8

A fourth mill, called the Washington, was started in Georgetown in November, 1867. It used six crucibles, each able to handle two tons of silver ore.

In 1864, the Mount Alpine Mining Company located its office in a small open piece of land south of Georgetown. A separate settlement grew up around their operation, and was named Elizabethtown in honor of Elizabeth Griffith. Several buildings were erected, and a swampy area filled with willows defined the boundary between Elizabethtown and Georgetown. As the two towns grew, this boundary became indistinguishable. Georgetown got its post office in 1866. The following year, the two towns agreed to merge under the Georgetown name. Elizabethtown had its own survey, and as for Georgetown, the original survey done by pioneer David Griffith had been lost. A new survey was done to neatly combine the two towns. A town charter was granted by the Territorial Legislature in 1868, and Georgetown became Clear Creek County's seat. From this point on, Georgetown was known as the "Silver Queen," and for decades to come, silver mining was its primary industry.

A train of jacks was a common sight on the streets of Georgetown. In this case, the animals each have a pair of rail destined for some area mine. This photograph is Rose Street looking south, and down the street is a hardware store, a bath house and an assay office. (Denver Public Library, Western History Department F7323)

Out of the four nineteenth century fire stations constructed in Georgetown, only this one, the Hope Hose No. 1, did not survive. It was located at the west end of 6th Street near the bridge over Clear Creek. (Colorado Historical Society F15672)

THE HANGING OF EDWARD BAINBRIDGE

As mining towns go, Georgetown was relatively quiet, and the number of violent crimes was quite small relative to other mining towns such as Creede or Leadville. There was one particular event, however, in April, 1867, which caused quite a stir. The town bully, Edward Bainbridge, threatened to shoot James Martin, a respected and quiet citizen of Georgetown. At the time of their first encounter, only the intervention of another man prevented the shooting.

Later, Bainbridge got Martin to agree to play poker for a can of oysters. Bainbridge even gave Martin the advantage of several points in a game which took place in a local saloon. Martin won the first hand easily, which irritated Bainbridge. The latter made a second threat to Martin's life; if he should win the second hand, Bainbridge would shoot him on the spot.

Apparently Martin did not take this threat seriously and won again. The last card had hardly touched the table's surface when Bainbridge drew and cocked his revolver. He placed it up against Martin's face and pulled the trigger. The explosion which followed sent the ball through Martin's nose and into the back of his brain. The flame from the black powder badly scorched Martin's face.

The wounded man fell over backward and was taken to a room where the local doctor pronounced his condition very serious and that he would probably die. He also said that the ball could not be removed. Amazingly, Martin remained lucid through this entire sequence of events and was able to relate to law officers exactly what had happened. Despite the severity of the wound, Martin eventually recovered and lived in Georgetown for many years.

In the meantime, the citizens of Georgetown became agitated over the premeditated attempted murder. Bainbridge was arrested immediately and escorted to a second story room with two officers standing guard on the lower floor.

Late that same evening, a large crowd surrounded the building as the officers tried to maintain control. Distracted by the mob, the officers did not notice a few men climbing up onto the second story roof. They broke a window to get inside. Once they located Bainbridge, they threw him out of a window onto the ground below. Other mob members immediately tied a clothesline around his neck. He was dragged to the nearest tree. The free end of the clothesline was tossed over a limb, and Bainbridge was hoisted by the neck and left to suffocate.

As expressed in *The Central City Register* the following morning, "To endorse such summary justice is not the part of a newspaper, but we cannot refrain from saying that Edward Bainbridge met a righteous fate."

Some accounts claim Bainbridge was the first occupant of the Georgetown cemetery. *The Georgetown Courier* told how his body was given to a Central City physician for dissection. It is also claimed that the skeleton of Edward Bainbridge eventually ended up in the hands of Dr. Irving J. Pollock, a well-known and well-liked pioneer physician in Georgetown. If true, Bainbridge finally served a useful purpose for society. Whenever Dr. Pollock needed to discuss human anatomy with a patient, he hauled out Edward's skeleton.

This should have ended the story. But later the same year, the owners of a home built on the site of the tree where Bainbridge was executed claimed that their house was haunted, forcing them to sell. The doors would fly open for no reason, even when locked, and the family said this was a nightly occurrence. After the house sold, no other reports of ghostly disturbances were made.

MINING MAGNATE WILLIAM HAMILL

William A. Hamill moved from Philadelphia to Central City in 1865 to run a cigar and tobacco store for his brother-in-law, Joseph Watson. The lure of quick riches through silver mining had brought Watson to Georgetown in 1866 and Hamill followed. A year later, Hamill moved his wife and two sons to Georgetown. In 1867, Watson constructed a modest home on the corner of Argentine and 3rd Street.

Watson ran into some bad luck with his own mining ventures and moved to Salt Lake City in 1871. Watson sold his home, and in the process, William Hamill became the owner.

William Hamill became one of the richest men in Colorado using a strategy of buying and selling mining property. He began to purchase undervalued claims on Brown Mountain about two and a half miles west of Georgetown and above Silver Plume. The tactic involved purchasing a claim adjacent to a productive mine and then forcing the mine into litigation. The Mining Law of 1872 encouraged this sort of strategy and could legally be used to bankrupt the owners of a productive mine. If the apex or highest point of a vein could be proven to lie within the boundaries of a claim, then all of the ore body below the surface could be mined. This was true even if the vein passed out of the sides of the claim. A person like Hamill could purchase a claim adjacent to a productive mine and begin tunneling right into the same vein, claiming that its apex was on his property. The courts would issue an injunction to stop all mining, and without revenue, the productive mine might be forced into bankruptcy. The owners, in some cases, took a mining expert like Hamill in as a partner!

By 1872, Hamill owned almost all or part of many silver claims on Brown Mountain. His personal wealth became sufficient to finance lengthy litigation. The one mine he did not have, however, was the British-owned Terrible Mine at the base of Brown Mountain. When Hamill became the manager of the Dives in 1875, he was also able to begin working on the Silver Ore mine next to the Terrible. He broke into the Terrible, and using the Apex Law, forced the Terrible into litigation and closure. The legal battle lasted from 1875 to 1877 preventing either mine from being worked profitably. The lower levels of the Terrible were at the center of the dispute, and the mine owners allowed these tunnels to flood.

Hamill and his partner, Jerome Chaffee, eventually forced the British company to buy them out for roughly a million dollars and consolidate the Terrible with the Silver Ore.

This is the Hamill House, owned and operated by Historic Georgetown Inc. as a museum. It represents the height of wealth and prosperity achieved by its owner, William Hamill. As Hamill's wealth grew, he added to the structure. Of particular note is the solarium on the left, made up of curved pieces of glass. (photograph by Kenneth Jessen)

Part of the payment to Hamill was a third interest in the consolidated property, which allowed Hamill to vote himself in as the manager. He was granted full managerial authority in 1879. He did, however, have to advance the company $30,000 to help liquidate its debt. Hamill did such a good job as manager, that by 1883, the company was able to pay its stockholders a dividend. The British, however, became fed up with Hamill's management style. Hamill reported to the board of directors only as he saw fit and ruled over the mining operations with an iron hand. The directors found it difficult to unseat a major stock holder and a member of their own board.

One large shareholder finally agreed to buy out William Hamill's stock, and in 1883, Hamill sent his son, Will, to London to complete the transaction. The shareholder had a change of mind and would not close the deal. Instead of returning to the United States, young Hamill borrowed against the shares and drank to excess for a year forcing his father to take legal action to retrieve the shares. Eventually the British company paid William Hamill approximately $22,000 for seven silver claims if he would, in turn, agree to leave.

The British formed a new mining company and began production. The tailings from the mine became so extensive that they began to bury a property called the Rainbow. Of all the bad luck, it was owned by Hamill who had the court slap an injunction on the British company forcing them to stop mining. This left the British paying Hamill an additional $75,000 to buy the Rainbow.

From 1874 to 1881, William Hamill used his wealth to transform the simple, two-story Watson home into the largest, most elegant mansion in Georgetown. He hired Denver architect Robert Roeschlaub to design the addition. It became a show place for Hamill's parties and a source of pride for Georgetown residents. In addition to expanding the house, two substantial buildings were added to the rear of the property. One was a large two-story carriage house, and the other was a two-and-a-half story office building.

Expensive furnishings, such as the mirrors over the fireplaces, were purchased. Camel's hair wallpaper was hung on the walls. In the library, an embossed leather-like wallpaper was used. Alternating strips of maple and walnut made up the parquet flooring. Possibly the most spectacular room in the mansion was the solarium, built in 1879. It was covered with curved panes of glass. Imported marble was used for the fireplace in the master bedroom. The exterior of the home was complimented by a beautiful lawn, garden, and shade trees surrounded by a low, decorative granite wall.

Although at times William Hamill and Jerome Chaffee were locked in litigation over the mineral rights on Brown Mountain, they eventually became partners. This may have been the beginning of Hamill's political interests, since Chaffee was an ardent Republican. During this time in Colorado history, mining and politics went hand in hand. Eventually, Hamill became a leader in the Republican Party and was elected to the state senate in 1876. He served as chairman of the State Republican Party and was seriously considered as a gubernatorial candidate. Later he would run for the U.S. Senate.

Hamill gave a great deal to the town of Georgetown. He was a civic leader and an investor in the town's future. Hamill was not universally liked, however, since some of the Georgetown's residents had been victims of his litigation over mining claims. Hamill paid to have the first flagstone sidewalk laid in front of his house and a hotel called The American House. This was a departure from the wooden sidewalks which dominated Georgetown. The Alpine House No. 2 wanted a fire bell, and Hamill paid all of the expenses, including transportation, for a 1200 pound bell which still hangs today in that firehouse. He also donated money to the local Catholic Church for a bell. The Grace Episcopal Church also got its bell courtesy of William Hamill.

In 1881, Hamill constructed a two-story brick building in downtown Georgetown. Known as the Hamill Block, it remains in use today on Rose Street between 5th and 6th streets. Other investments included a ranch in Middle Park, a farm near Denver, and a wagon road over Berthoud Pass.

Sometimes called "General" Hamill, he was named Brigadier-General in the state militia by Colorado Governor Pitkin after the Ute Indian uprising in 1879 on the White River Agency. During this time, he made field trips to insure that the Indians remained confined to their reservation. No conflict occurred.

This chateau-style building, located at the rear of the Hamill House, was built in 1879 to serve as William Hamill's office. (photograph by Kenneth Jessen)

At one time, Hamill was part owner of *The Denver Tribune* and also loaned Jesse Summers Randall money needed to start *The Georgetown Courier* in 1877. Both men wanted a local paper with a Republican slant. The loan was later repaid by Randall

William Hamill raised four sons and a daughter in his Georgetown house. His fortunes were closely tied to the price of silver. When the Sherman Silver Purchase Act was repealed in 1893, the market for silver

16

This is the carriage house and stable, located behind the Hamill House and built in 1879. The carriage house and office building were designed by Denver architect Robert Roeschlaub. (photograph by Kenneth Jessen)

declined sharply along with William Hamill's wealth. He moved to Denver and passed away in 1904. One of his sons, Tom, continued to live in the Hamill House. Tom worked as Georgetown's postmaster until 1914, when he and his family moved away.

Historic Georgetown Inc. purchased the Hamill House in 1971 and began an extensive restoration project. They have spent an estimated half million dollars on its restoration and keep the house open to the public for tours.

Even the privy behind the Hamill House was unusual with its own ornate Victorian appearance. Note the scroll-work over the entrance, the clapboard siding and the cupola on the roof. (photograph by Kenneth Jessen)

17

The Alpine Hose No. 2 is often used as Georgetown's symbol, and rightly so, since it was the volunteer fire departments that kept fire damage to a minimum and preserved the town. This building was constructed in 1875, shortly after Georgetown was organized into four fire protection zones. In 1880, wealthy mine owner William Hamill purchased a bell, and the sixty-foot bell tower at the rear of the structure was built. (photograph by Kenneth Jessen)

FIRE DEPARTMENT SAVES TOWN

Fortunately for Georgetown and those that visit today, the need for a good fire department was recognized early in the town's history. This explains why so many nineteenth century, wood-frame buildings survive. The town board met in 1868 to put together a committee to organize bucket brigades and fire lanes from town to the nearest source of water. Georgetown did have the advantage of two creeks running through town.

In 1869, the first fire company was organized and money was raised to purchase a fire engine (pulled by the firemen), 300 feet of hose and 50 buckets. By using fourteen men to operate the pump (seven per side), this engine could produce a steam of water reaching 130 feet. A devastating fire in 1871 destroyed the Barton House, a popular hotel, and put men and equipment to the test. A combination fire station and town hall was completed in 1873 on the west end of 6th Street where it crosses Clear Creek. The need for a water works with fire hydrants was brought home when nearly every structure in Central City was leveled by the fire of 1874. Instead of long hoses running from the closest creek, short hoses to the nearest hydrant could be used. This system was made operational in 1874, and at the same time, the Hope Hose Company No. 1 was started. The Alpine Hose Company No. 2 soon followed.

In 1875, two new fire houses were constructed: the Alpine Hose Company No. 2 on 5th Street and the Old Missouri fire house on Taos Street occupied by the Georgetown Fire and Hose Company No. 1. The Hope Hose Company No. 1 and the Star Hook and Ladder Company jointly occupied the original combination fire state and town hall. In 1881, the Star Hook and Ladder Company moved to a building directly across 6th Street from the Hotel de Paris and in 1886, constructed their own quarters. With the exception of the Hope Hose Company No. 1, all of these fire stations remain standing today.

The bells used to call the volunteers and to alert citizens of a fire were difficult to hear. Mine owner and civic leader William Hamill offered to purchase a new and louder bell for the Alpine Hose building. A tower was constructed, and the bell was put into service in 1880. It was said that even those hard of hearing could hear this bell!

By 1886, statistics show that Georgetown had 193 firemen, a number of hose carts, a hook and ladder truck plus 3,500 feet of hose.

Humans could respond faster than horses to a fire call, so all of the carts and trucks were pulled by the firemen. This required good physical strength and conditioning. Using shoulder harnesses, a typical fire truck was pulled by nine volunteers plus four more at the wheels.

The volunteer firemen were possibly the best conditioned men in town. It was not long before these volunteer companies were pitted against each other in various contests. The 4th of July was selected for the annual races between fire companies in Georgetown. A track was built and spectators sat in a grand stand. The Colorado State Firemen's Tournament was held in Georgetown in 1886, and several new records were set during the event.

The following year, the volunteer firemen were called out to stop a blaze at the Fish Block, at Rose and 6th Street, which could have easily leveled the entire town. As it was, the Bank of Clear Creek County and a saloon were reduced to ashes.

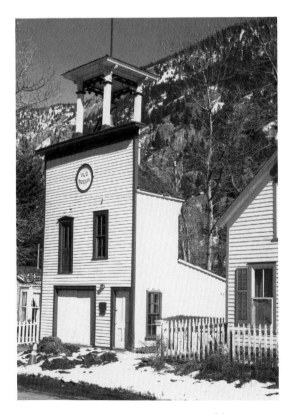

Facing west toward Georgetown's park is the Old Missouri Firehouse. This was once the home of The Georgetown Fire and Hose Company No. 1. The building was constructed in 1875 and was originally a one-story structure which was enlarged to include a second story, a bell tower and a balcony. (photograph by Kenneth Jessen)

In 1867, Erskine McClellan built the McClellan Hall with a theater on the second floor and a furniture store and carpenter shop on the first floor. On a cold winter night in 1892, the pipes in the building froze. McClellan built a small fire under the pipes to get them thawed. The fire got out of control and spread into the wood shavings used as insulation between the inner and outer walls. McClellan summoned the fire department, and in short order, 5,000 feet of hose was pressed into use. The first hoses laid by the firemen froze, but once the hoses thawed and the walls of the building fell, the fire department was able to contain the blaze. The hall was totally destroyed, and the American House and several other downtown structures were badly damaged. The plate glass windows on a photo gallery and a drug store broke under the intense heat. The Hotel de Paris, adjacent to McClellan Hall, was scorched and the entire business district would have been lost if it hadn't been for Georgetown's volunteer fire department.

The Star Hook and Ladder Company is yet another fine example of a Georgetown fire house. This building was constructed in 1886 and was designed for a long truck equipped with a ladder. (photograph by Kenneth Jessen)

Jesse Summers Randall constructed what began as a very modest home in 1876, but as his business and his family grew, he added and modified the structure. Today, it looks very much as it did in 1885. (photograph by Kenneth Jessen)

Shown with his mineral collection, Jesse Summers Randall was founder and publisher of The Georgetown Courier. *Randall was born in Kentucky and died in Georgetown in 1939 at the age of 91. (Colorado Historical Society, F15829)*

EDITOR JESSE SUMMERS RANDALL

Towns are made not only by their merchants, teachers, preachers and business people, but also by those who report the news. Georgetown was blessed with many good newspaper editors during its history, but best remembered is Jesse Summers Randall. When Jesse Randall first arrived in Georgetown in 1869, he was already experienced in the newspaper business. He became the plant foreman for *The Colorado Miner,* Georgetown's first newspaper. The *Miner* started as a weekly, changed to an evening daily, then returned to a weekly due to lack of support from advertisers and subscribers. Subscriptions, by the way, were just $4 per year.

The editorial direction of the *Miner* was as simple as its name; the paper was devoted to coverage of the mining industry and enjoyed wide circulation throughout the Territory of Colorado. In its later years, it supported the Democratic Party.

What initially brought Jesse to Georgetown was his father, Abram Randall. Abram's doctor told him to leave his Kentucky home and move to a high, dry mountain climate. His move to Georgetown proved to be excellent advice since Abram lived to be 101 years old.

After six years, Jesse Randall left his job with the *Miner* and purchased a small hand press and opened a job printing shop. His experience with the *Miner* had left him with knowledge of how to run a newspaper, but little to show financially. Part of his motivation for leaving the *Miner* may have been his marriage to an Iowa girl in 1874. The marriage took place after a lengthy courtship by mail, beginning when Randall arrived in Georgetown.

Georgetown had grown quickly to about 5,000 residents and was a busy place with its economy almost solely based on silver mining. The demand for job printing was great, and Jesse did well. In just two years, combined with a loan from wealthy miner owner William Hamill, Randall had enough money to begin publication of his own newspaper, *The Georgetown Courier.* He purchased the old Washington hand press used by the *Miner* when that paper decided to modernize. This press, along with its moveable type, had been brought across the prairie and was first used by the pioneer *Rocky Mountain News.* It then came up Clear Creek Canyon in a covered wagon to serve the *Miner* during its first years.

The first edition of the *Courier* was printed May 24, 1877. The newspaper office was located in the Fish Block at Alpine and Rose streets. Soon, Randall moved the *Courier* to a false-front, one-story frame building near the corner of Alpine and Taos. This building became known as the Courier Building, and the newspaper remained at the same location for the rest of its publication life.

Eventually Randall modernized and replaced the old hand press with a powered press. The printing press and other equipment in the office was powered by a Backus Water Motor which contained a Pelton wheel. The Pelton wheel was driven by water pressure from Georgetown's water main, and belts throughout the building were used to distribute the power to various pieces of equipment.

The format Randall selected for his newspaper was very large; the paper measured twenty-two inches by twenty-eight inches. It had nine columns per page, and each of the early issues had four pages.

As a side line, Jesse Randall used his extensive knowledge of mineralogy to sell collections of fifty to one hundred minerals with prices ranging from $3.00 to $10.00. He also wrote a book titled *The Mineralogy of Colorado*. Randall retained his job printing business and advertised that he could handle book printing, business cards, invitations, and so on.

Jesse Summers Randall was known as "the fighting editor" for his stand on ethics. During the 1880s, he may have been caught up in a reform movement which spread across the United States. This may have led to the feud with William Hamill, the very same man who loaned Randall the money to get the *Courier* started. The details of their conflict vary considerably according to the source. Randall felt that Georgetown's leading citizens should set an example for the rest of the town.

Hamill's son, Will, was a heavy drinker and did not assume responsibility for his father's business dealings, causing William Hamill some embarrassment. One evening in 1884, Will got into a street brawl. The officer who attempted to arrest Will was badly beaten. This was just the type of behavior Randall hated, and this led to an attack by the *Courier* critical of William Hamill's parental abilities.

The *Miner*, seeing that Hamill was defenseless, came to the rescue. Although the *Miner* supported the Democrats and Hamill was a Republican, the newspaper defended Hamill in many of its issues and counterattacked Randall. Referring to Randall, but not by name, they wrote, "We know of a newspaper...that was kindly assisted in financial difficulties by

24

a public-spirited citizen...No sooner was this situation attained that it did, snake-like, turn upon its benefactor."

James Blaine was chosen as the Republican nominee for the 1884 presidential election, and Hamill was sent to the Republican National Convention in Chicago to represent Colorado. The *Miner* reported on how well Hamill did his job, much to the annoyance of Randall. Randall could easily have believed that the Republicans were rewarding bad behavior.

The *Miner* attacked again calling Randall a "mangy human cur." Hamill lost his patience when Randall went so far as to accused him of fraternizing with the Democrats. Hamill filed a law suit against Randall on August 30, 1884, not for slander, but to recover nearly two thousand dollars in unpaid debts he claimed Randall owed him. The court settlement was for a little over two hundred dollars.

One of Randall's accounts described Hamill as going to any lengths to secure the 1880 Republican nomination for the U.S. Senate. Randall claimed Hamill held the Republican convention in the Georgetown Courthouse to insure success. To eliminate any threat to his nomination, Hamill had a local blacksmith fashion steel straps on the inside of the courthouse doors. This allowed 2x4's to be slid through the straps. Behind these closed, locked doors with only his close friends on hand, Hamill received the nomination.

Randall supplied his readers with all the details of Hamill's underhanded scheme. His article presumably caused a landslide victory for the Democrats filling all county offices. According to Randall, Hamill retaliated by calling for a boycott of the *Courier*.

After the Alpine Hose Company won the hose races in 1877, they celebrated using "Little Nellie," a parade cannon. According to Randall, the cannon was pointed at the *Courier* office, fired repeatedly, and broke all of its windows.

Randall prevailed and continued to publish *The Georgetown Courier.* Hamill, on the other hand, eventually went broke, but only after he constructed Georgetown's largest and most elegant mansion.

Jesse Randall continued as the editor/owner of the *Courier* for many years and generously donated a great deal of information to the Colorado Historical Society. He passed away at the age of 91.

After his death, Jesse's son Neal ran the *Courier* until 1948, when poor health forced him to retire. The paper continued until 1958.

The legal fraternity of Georgetown is gathered in this 1874 photograph in front of the office of John H. McMurdy. Edward Wolcott is standing to the left of the tall gentleman with the top hat. The building was once the post office and ended up as Wolcott's office. (Colorado Historical Society F4061)

Edward O. Wolcott had sort of a boyish look about him and parted his blond hair almost in the middle. He was about twenty-five when this photograph was taken. (Colorado Historical Society F12409)

EDWARD WOLCOTT BECOMES U.S. SENATOR

Arriving in Georgetown during Christmas week of 1871, Edward Oliver Wolcott wanted to begin his career as a lawyer. He had been teaching school in Black Hawk for several months and decided to join lawyer Frank Pope. The sign over Pope's place of business soon was changed to read "Pope & Wolcott - Attorneys and Counselors at Law."

Wolcott had blue eyes, blond hair and a thick, blond mustache. He came from a cultured, New England family of Congregational clergymen and Colonial governors. In fact, one of his ancestors, Oliver Wolcott, signed the Declaration of Independence. Wolcott spent part of a year at Yale and completed his law degree at the Harvard Law School.

"Judge" Pope, Wolcott's partner, was a Southern gentleman, a ladies man, and not especially fond of work. Pope seemed to be content living off of an income of $2,500 per year.

Colorado law required Wolcott to work as an apprentice before he could appear in court. It was, however, difficult to make a living. Limited income forced Wolcott to sleep in his one room office on Alpine Street using a table as a bed. In the morning, he stowed the bed-clothing out of sight. He was not especially sociable and seldom attended social functions. Never seen in the company of a woman, some regarded him as not the marrying kind. He would, however, escort married women to social functions when their husbands were out of town on business or women whose husbands who did not want to attend. Many of Georgetown's wives were married to older men, and Wolcott somehow fit the role of escort for these women.

Wolcott was not devoid of humor, however. He did engage in practical jokes such as "snipe hunts" and was often seen playing billiards. He also had a passion for fine clothes.

In 1872, Wolcott wrote his father that Georgetown had fourteen lawyers for a population of 2,000 individuals. Times, he said, were hard because the prices on mining property were inflated relative to their true value due to speculation. He went on to state that overcapitalization prevented a fair return for investors.

As soon as he completed his apprenticeship, Wolcott parted company with Pope and opened his own office. In 1873, Edward Wolcott tried his hand as a part-time editor of *The Colorado Miner*, but lasted only three months. After a full day of work and a good meal, Wolcott would show up at the newspaper office only to doze off at his desk. The printer would be sent to Wolcott's office just before the paper was due to go to press and stir Wolcott out of his slumber to get his work. Wolcott's typical response was to throw what ever was handy at the printer.

Being an editor forced Wolcott to socialize, since this is how a newspaper editor on the frontier gathered the news. By visiting the saloons, Wolcott learned much about human nature and became friends with many of Georgetown's pioneers. This activity also led to heavy drinking, and on several occasions, Wolcott had to be carried to his bed in the corner of his office by his friends. When it looked like Wolcott's life and career were on a downhill slide, his friends gathered enough money to send him on a long trip to Japan to sober up. After his return, he never drank heavily again.

Until 1876, Edward Wolcott had shown no interest in local politics. His private practice was barely profitable, and there were doubts that he even liked being an attorney. He especially disliked court proceedings and avoided situations where he had to appear before a jury. His brother Henry, and prominent mill owner Nathaniel Hill, were deeply involved in the Republican Party politics and had faith in Edward's talent. Local party leaders, like William Hamill, had their doubts and could not see Edward as an effective speaker.

Despite these feelings, Edward Wolcott was elected District Attorney and also accepted the job of Georgetown's Town Attorney. Most of his pay was based on court proceedings, and Wolcott's solution to this was to send his assistant.

Local residents felt Wolcott was easy on criminals and that he handed out light sentences. They wanted a DA who would string up those who deserved to be strung up. As explained by local defense lawyer Morrison, concerning Wolcott's court manners, "His abilities...seemed to be entirely neutralized and rendered worthless by a reluctance to appear in court." Wolcott was often the object of contempt among other lawyers.

Edward Wolcott was a generous man, however. A stage driver named Hi Washburn was involved in a rollover accident below Georgetown in 1873. Dr. Collins and Dr. Pollock were forced to amputate Washburn's leg. This left Washburn few options as to how to make a living; in a mining town, only able-bodied men were hired. Wolcott apparently felt sorry for the former stage coach driver and sent him a monthly allowance for the remainder his life.

A turning point came in Wolcott's career when he was given a murder case. The two men who stood accused were represented by his local critic, Morrison. As his associate, Wolcott used a student. Toward the end of the trial, the defense charged Wolcott with coaching two young boys on how to respond when on the witness stand. In a speech, Wolcott forcefully and flatly denied the charges and went on to say that the only coaching he gave the boys was to tell the truth in their own words. This must have been a most convincing speech since the jury rendered the verdict of first degree murder against both defendants. Later, it was noted that the verdict was more severe than the evidence would support, and one of the defendants was later pardoned.

Apparently from this point on, Wolcott's fear of talking publicly vanished. It might also be noted that Wolcott talked at the rate of about two hundred words a minute, so fast that court recorders could hardly keep up. All in all, Edward Wolcott turned out to be a successful District Attorney, and during his term in office, never lost a case. After his term of office ended, his private practice began to pick up.

In 1878 at the age of thirty, Edward Wolcott left Georgetown to start a practice in Denver. By this time, he had gained some weight and parted his fair hair in the middle. He became more self-reliant, more at ease around people and, consequently, a better speaker. He got interested in politics and eventually became a U.S. Senator from Colorado.

His brother Henry joined Edward in Denver where they rented a large house which allowed them to entertain. Henry was thrifty, methodical and temperate. Ed was more impulsive and dressed in striped trousers complimented by a fawn-colored waistcoat. The two bachelors made an interesting pair.

Edward's practice continued to improve, as evidenced by a $15,000 retainer from the Denver & Rio Grande Railroad to represent their interests. He lived out his life in comfort.

The offices of the Dives and Pelican Mining Company and the Western Union Telegraph Company were in the same building. The feud between the Dives and Pelican ended in 1880, after seven years. This building is still standing and is located on Taos Street between 5th and 6th streets. (Denver Public Library, Western History Department F5136)

THE UNDERGROUND FEUD

The feud between the owners of two claims, the Pelican and Dives, high above Silver Plume, was of such significance that the Colorado Historical Society devoted an entire book to the subject. It was authored by noted Georgetown historian Liston Leyendecker, Professor of History at Colorado State University, and titled *The Pelican-Dives Feud*.

The mining legislation of 1872 included the Apex Law. It permitted the owner of a mining claim the exclusive right to work all veins and ore bodies throughout the entire length of a claim if the apex or highest point of the vein were within the claim's rectangular limits of 600 feet by 1,500 feet. If the vein strayed out of the claim somewhere deep underground, the owner could follow the vein literally to the center of the earth as long as it passed through the sides of the claim and not its ends.

Such a law was made for the legal profession and was the ruin of many good silver mines in the Georgetown area. Litigation nearly always occurred between the "haves" and "have-nots." For example, the owner of a claim with low grade ore could challenge the owner of a rich lode. The first thing the courts would do was slap an injunction on both claims until the issue was settled, thus halting all production. Challengers often brought suit as a form of legal extortion to force the owners of a bonanza to buy them out. In many cases, the profits of an otherwise rich mine would be eaten up fighting court battles. This tended to turn away investors who could have materially helped in the development of a potentially rich mine.

Low grade ore, possibly not even worth the effort to mine, could surface on a given claim from some point deep within the earth. The owner of that claim could file suit against the owners of a nearby productive mine. This would be especially true if the low grade ore surfaced at a point higher than the rich vein. The court battle could take years to resolve because of insufficient data as to whether or not the low grade ore body ever joined the rich vein. For the mine owners, it was often cheaper to simply buy the worthless claim and pay off its owner.

Eli Streeter and Thomas McCunniff, plus several others, hardly expected to strike it rich some 800 feet above Cherokee Gulch on the steep side of Republican Mountain during 1870. The two men started work on what was called the Pelican during the summer of 1871. They dug a series of adits into the side of Republican Mountain which permitted exploration of the ore body and ore extraction. The proposition paid for itself in that the ore mined during exploration yielded the necessary funding to continue.

In June, 1872, they struck a rich ore body 1,400 feet long. By now, some sixty men had been hired for the work in two shifts. McCunniff boasted he would have his men work through the winter of 1872-73. By the summer of 1874, four tunnels had been opened, and employment grew to one hundred miners.

The Colorado Miner told of great wealth within the Pelican in several issues and also how handsome the profits were for its owners. The net yield, for example, from January 1, 1872 to the following June, was $175,000. In 1873, the *Miner* claimed that the Pelican was the richest mine in the state with ore running between 800 and 1,000 ounces of pure silver per ton.

The owners took on new partners, and of note was Jacob Snider. He was experienced at mining and milling. Snider became involved with the Pelican when he began crushing its ore in a Silver Plume mill he supervised. In 1874, he purchased an interest in the Pelican. During the feud, Snider was shot to death by Jackson Bishop and became a casualty of the Pelican-Dives feud. (see "Jackson Bishop The Outlaw")

Thomas Burr staked out the Dives claim in 1869 and sold an interest to William A. Hamill the following July. Hamill was an entrepreneur who made part of his living through the blackmail allowed by litigation using the Apex Law. The Dives had the potential of becoming a very rich property with assay results running as high as 680 ounces of silver per ton. The ore body became richer as the mine increased in depth. The Dives was situated to the southeast of the Pelican and at not too great a distance with part of its claim crossing part of the Pelican's claim.

In 1873, the owners of the Dives were being rewarded with high grade ore running as much as 700 ounces of silver per ton. The vein was two feet thick. By 1874, the rich seam had dwindled to just a few inches.

Since both mines were producing good ore, they attracted numerous outside investors who purchased pieces of the properties at inflated prices.

A dispute began between the owners of the contiguous Elkhorn and Zillah lodes. A couple of prospectors discovered rich silver ore in a crevice and staked out the Zillah lode in 1868. Other prospectors claimed another lode adjacent to the Zillah which they called the Elkhorn. As these lodes were mined, it became obvious that they were one and the same. The dispute which erupted was settled in 1872 with the consolidation of the properties. When underground operations were expanding in the Pelican, the owners of the Zillah claimed that the Pelican was infringing on the same vein. They said that they had title to all of this vein by virtue of the Apex Law. This forced the owners of the Pelican to buy out the owners of the Zillah to avoid litigation.

The Pelican owners filed a new law suit against the Dives. No less than twenty-three law suits followed during the feud between these properties. The battle lines then shifted underground; the owners of the Dives cut into the Zillah Lode, consolidated in ownership with the Pelican. They dug twenty-three feet lower than active mining by the Pelican and took out a great deal of rich ore. The Dives owners claimed they were simply following the same vein on which their original claim was made. Eventually the two mining companies were mining above and below each other endangering each other's employees. An injunction stopped progress.

The actual legal dispute between the Pelican and the Dives began in December, 1873, and started with the relatively simple complaint of trespass against the Perdue Silver and Gold Mining and Ore Reducing Company. The latter was the lessee of the Dives claim. The owners of the Pelican charged that the Perdue owners sank a discovery shaft in the crevice of the Bell Weather Lode, also owned by the Pelican. They also charged the Perdue company with drilling into the Zillah Lode.

The outcome of the approaching trial was very important to Georgetown residents since their lives and occupations depended on silver mining. *The Georgetown Courier* noted that the courtroom was a walking arsenal and that the judge had as his "advisors," two large revolvers. The judge agreed to a change of venue to El Paso County, and when the arguments were heard, among other things, the judge pointed out that the patent (title) for the Zillah was faulty.

Streeter and McCunniff, owners of the Pelican, had to prove in court that they occupied the disputed ground first and that the disputed vein was actually separate from the rest of the Dives. Streeter and McCunniff won this round, and an injunction was issued against the Perdue company which prohibited them from mining within thirty feet of the Zillah lode.

Naturally, a counter suit was filed by the Perdue company in the form of a statement which attempted to establish a prior claim on its lodes. They also pointed out that they had spent $50,000 on the discovery shaft and that Streeter and McCunniff had never objected. It was also argued by the Perdue company that Streeter and McCunniff received a patent (title) to the Zillah without having performed the required $1,000 in improvements.

The Perdue company added a grievance that told how a large number of Pelican miners had illegally entered the Dives 160 feet below the surface and removed large quantities of rich silver ore. The Perdue company pointed out that its own mining activity was confined only to ore which was part of the Dives claim. It sought a half a million dollars in damages for ore illegally removed by the Pelican.

As for the ore which was removed, the Perdue company tried to get an injunction against the owners of the Pelican to prevent them from processing ore stored at various locations. There was no practical means of accurately determining what ore had been removed and from what lode. The ambiguity of the situation allowed the legal wizards to make their money at the expense of the mine owners. One thing was certain, both the Pelican and Dives companies were trying to extract rich silver ore from the very same location under the earth's surface.

The only recourse for the court was to enter the mining business itself. The judge ordered that a winz, or steep incline, be sunk in the disputed area. The winz defined the vein and which way it ran. This mining operation by the court did not break into either property. As a result, the court ordered the Perdue company to erect a gate at the end of its drift where it entered the workings of the opposing company. The gate was to be kept locked except for inspection purposes. In the three dimensional world of mining, gates are of little consequence, and both the Dives and Pelican kept on mining rich silver ore in the disputed area.

Very little survey work had been done in Colorado, and when it came to the actual physical location of the Zillah, the boundary was quite vague. It was referenced relative to a small ravine called Cherokee Gulch, and land records were used to define the exact location of the discovery shaft.

The legal battle continued throughout 1873. To continue to extract ore, the Perdue company would begin mining the Dives at midnight on Saturday and work for twenty-four hours. The ore was transported down the mountain side and hidden. The Perdue company paid extremely high wages to its miners and demanded their secrecy. They also hired armed guards to protect the mine and the ore. This type of operation lasted several weeks and resulted in the removal of $65,000 in ore which was taken to Georgetown. Under the cover of darkness, it was transported to Black Hawk for processing. When questioned, the Dives management simply said that the ore stored in Georgetown had been stolen.

The feud between the Pelican and Dives was not without its humor, however. Deputy Sheriff P. C. Baily was instructed to commandeer ore coming from the Dives. When he saw one of their covered wagons, typically used for transporting high-grade ore, he intercepted it and ordered the driver to take it down to a Georgetown stable. At the stable, a crowd gathered to see what would happen. Baily ordered the cover unlocked, and the driver refused. When it became clear that Baily was going to break the lock, the driver acted out his role perfectly and relented. When the lid was opened, the surprised sheriff found two miners inside and no ore! The miners stood up in the wagon much to the delight of the crowd. In the meantime, an open ore wagon, full of rich ore from the Dives, passed the stable and went to a local mill where the ore was deposited.

After the court ruled in favor of the Pelican owners, the injunction was lifted and mining resumed. The settlement, however, allowed the Dives miners to work one particular drift which the Pelican sought for itself. On the night of April 24, 1875, a force of armed men from the Pelican broke into the lower portion of the Dives. When the Dives miners returned to work in the morning, they set off one blast to release ore. The miners from the Pelican had been waiting in their connecting tunnel and took possession of the Dives by force. This allowed the Pelican to work a rich section of the Dives, and needless to say, another round of legal battles was touched off.

Along with a force of around two hundred men working both mines, another twenty or so well-armed men stood guard duty on the surface. The two mines were within easy rifle shot of each other. All visitors were denied access to the area. A Central City judge issued an injunction against the Pelican, and Deputy Sheriff P. C. Baily rode up to deliver a writ to the defendants. He was shot at for his attempt, and the men at the Pelican said they would resist any attempt by Baily and his posse to enter the mine. Baily backed off and posted men at what he believed were all the mine openings in hopes of starving out the Pelican invaders. Using an obscure tunnel, food and water were smuggled into the Pelican's men.

During the standoff, a watchman in the Pelican left his post to get a drink of water and slipped and fell several feet down a steep incline. He was carrying a loaded pistol in his hand, and it accidentally discharged, killing him.

Baily had his problems. Not only was he denied access to the Pelican, he was also sent threatening notes from their attorney, Central City lawyer Henry Teller. The first such note ended with "...the Pelican people will be justified in defending their property, if they are compelled to kill you and your posse." A second note said "...and if Streeter and McCunniff serve you right, they will shoot you and your men like dogs." Teller refused to give up the ground mentioned in the writ and simply defied the law. The frustrated Baily then kidnapped one of the Pelican's officers right out of his Georgetown office. He placed the surprised man in a buggy with three armed posse members and hauled him up to the mine. The posse tried to use this man as a human shield, but the men guarding the mine apparently were willing to sacrifice one of their own if necessary.

Pressure was placed on the lawyers to settle the feud once and for all. The reputation of Georgetown as a sophisticated, law-abiding town had been shattered. Its population had been polarized between the two factions. After the legal community had been paid an estimated half a million dollars over a period of years, the Dives and Pelican owners finally agreed to stop their legal proceeding against each other. Eventually, in 1880, William Hamill consolidated the claims and helped with the formation of the Dives and Pelican Mining Company. Some owners lost, others gained, but the biggest winners in the Pelican-Dives feud were the lawyers.

JACKSON BISHOP THE OUTLAW

The dark-haired, blue-eyed Jackson Bishop looked on as Deputy Sheriff P. C. Baily was unable to serve a warrant against the owners of the Pelican Mine high above Silver Plume. Bloodshed would have resulted had the sheriff pressed the issue against the armed guards. Jackson Bishop was a miner and one of the lessees of a portion of the Dives which was locked in legal combat with the Pelican. He was also a member of a gang of thugs that harassed many of Georgetown's citizens, and historians have even said he was a hired gun.

Jackson Bishop's past records indicated a life of violence and a disrespect for authority. After being captured by Union soldiers during the Civil War, he pledged allegiance to the Union Army. He became a model soldier and eventually was not guarded. As soon the opportunity came along, however, he deserted the ranks and joined the Confederate Quantrill's Raiders.

He moved to Georgetown after the war with his brother Samuel and was joined by two other brothers. He owned a cottage in Georgetown and was married.

Jackson was hired in 1873 by the owners of the Phoenix mine to eject the miners at the Main. The feud was typical of Colorado mines where claims overlapped. Jackson was one of a dozen armed men who took control of the Main by force. During the struggle, one of the Main's miners was shot and killed. After his arrest and release on bail, Jackson Bishop and the other gang members were acquitted. Speculation was that the jury members felt threatened by Bishop's gang and feared retaliation.

City Marshal William Jacobs did not yield to the terror tactics Jackson Bishop and his gang inflicted on the town. One day, Bishop made out his final will and began cleaning his revolvers for a showdown with Jacobs. Jackson made death threats against the marshal who was advised to stay off the streets. Instead, Jacobs prepared himself for combat. At the end of the day, Bishop backed down and went home to bed.

A great deal of litigation took place trying to settle the ownership of a vein of rich silver ore under the Pelican and Dives lodes. Beneath the two claims, the veins of silver ore joined, making the matter of ownership of the lode a difficult legal proposition. Jackson and his gang blew open a crosscut and forcibly prevented the Pelican miners from working this part

37

of their claim. Even though the Dives side of the dispute seemed to be winning in court, Bishop believed things were not moving along fast enough.

The Pelican kept on operating, hauling out tons of rich silver ore. Deputy Sheriff Baily was sent up with a posse to serve an injunction on the Pelican to prevent further mining. Bishop asked to go along, but Baily denied his request considering Bishop too volatile and hot-headed. Bishop rode along anyway. He watched the futile attempt by Baily to serve the writ, and felt that Baily was not assertive enough and backed down too easily. The posse retreated without having performed its duties.

This incident angered Jackson Bishop, and he commented that there appeared to be no law in the Georgetown area for others or himself. At first, Bishop seemed content to ride back to Georgetown with the rest of the posse, then suddenly drew a revolver and headed back up toward the mines, shouting that he intended to take the law into his own hands. On the way up the road, he threatened several people irrespective of their connection with the Pelican or the Dives dispute.

The owners of the Pelican took on a new partner, Jacob Snider. He arrived in the Georgetown area sometime in 1863 and had experience in the California Gold Rush. He knew mining and milling. In 1866, he was the superintendent of the Snider Gold Mining Company of Philadelphia. They had a water-driven mill near Mill City (now known as Dumont). Snider formed a new company, the Trenton Gold and Silver Mining Company, and worked lodes in the Georgetown area.

The Trenton company constructed a crushing mill about two miles west of Georgetown on the future site of Silver Plume. Snider's firm built the first homes in Silver Plume. He became involved with the Pelican by taking its ore and crushing it in his mill. The Pelican looked like a good investment to him, and in 1874, he purchased an interest in the Pelican.

During the feud, Jacob Snider kept an eye on what was happening at the mines. He reported his findings by telegraph to Henry Teller in Central City who represented the Pelican. After sending a succession of three messages about Baily's unsuccessful attempt to serve a writ, Snider went to the livery stable to rent a horse. Unarmed, he headed up the road toward the mines when he met Jackson Bishop. Bishop was in no mood to deal with any one associated with the Pelican, especially a spy. Snider sensed that Bishop had gone insane, so he wheeled his horse around and galloped back toward Georgetown. Bishop was right behind Snider, riding at a full gallop with a revolver in one hand.

Bishop fired once as Snider crossed the bridge over Clear Creek, but missed. Snider tried to enter the livery stable at Alpine and Rose where he hoped to take cover, but a buggy blocked the way. This gave Bishop a chance to get close enough to strike Snider on the back of the head with the butt of his pistol. Snider fell to the ground with one foot still stuck in the stirrup. Bishop flipped his Colt Navy cap-and-ball revolver in his hand and fired at point blank range at the helpless man. The ball when into Snider's brain, killing him instantly. Bishop wheeled his horse around and galloped toward the Pelican-Divers mines. The murder was witnessed by a number of Georgetown residents.

Not far up the road, Jackson Bishop came across a wagon with his brother, Sam, sitting in the back. Deputy Sheriff King and one the Pelican's owners were on the front seat. Bishop, pointed his revolver at the mine owner and said, "I've just killed Jake Snider. I shot him. Yes, I shot him through the head, and his brains spattered out on the floor." Bishop threatened to do the same to the mine owner while the deputy was fearful that if he tried to arrest Jackson, his brother Sam might shoot him in the back.

Suddenly, Bishop changed his mind, decided that the mine owner was a gentleman, and continued riding toward the mines. Bishop rode up the switchbacks, past the Dives and on to the Denver Lode where he could watch all the activity below. A miner was home in a cabin near the Denver and later reported that Bishop demanded food and was armed with no less than six revolvers and a repeating rifle.

While he ate, Bishop spied on the Pelican. He mistook axes for rifles in the hands of two men who appeared to be coming up the hill toward him. He knew he was a wanted man, but would put up a good fight. He hid behind a rock intent on an ambush until he realized that the men were only unarmed miners. He let the men pass and went down to where he could watch the boarding house at the Pelican. As dusk approached, he took pot shots at the men inside. No one was hit, but one man had a bullet pass through his shirt.

Jackson Bishop then rode over Union Pass to Empire. The trees along the bank of the creek below Empire hid him from view and allowed him to enter town unnoticed. At the Lindstrom Brewery, Bishop dismounted and went in to visit the bartender, Harry Carns. He told Carns his story, and

Carns hid Bishop's horse in a dense clump of willows. He had Bishop lie down between the big vats.

Carns saw Deputy Sheriff John Devotie approaching, and the bartender acted half asleep as the deputy entered the brewery. The law officer asked if he had seen Bishop, and Carns responded by telling the absolute truth! He said that the fugitive was hiding behind the row of big vats in the cellar. The deputy, however, knew that Carns was a habitual liar, and since the vats were in plain sight, the lawman did not take the matter seriously. The deputy drank a glass of beer and left.

Carns hid Bishop for a week and provided the outlaw with blankets and food. The brewery owner's wife eventually became suspicious, especially since food was missing, but said nothing. Well after Bishop had left for Middle Park, she lifted a plate, discovering enough money to pay for the missing food.

Jackson Bishop remained in Middle Park and surrounded himself with a dozen or so friends. He defied Clear Creek County law officers to come and get him. What ultimately happened to Jackson Bishop is unknown, but he was never captured and brought to trial for the murder of Jacob Snider.

DECATUR'S DUAL LIFE

Stephen Decatur Bross, second son of Joseph Bross, was born in Sussex, New Jersey. Stephen learned the shoe making trade from his father. He attended several terms at Williams College in Massachusetts, went on to become a teacher and worked his way up to principal of an academy in New York. After his marriage, a daughter was born, and it seemed like a wonderfully normal life was in store for Stephen.

Just before the war with Mexico broke out, Stephen Decatur Bross went to New York City on business and vanished. His wife and relatives made great efforts to find him and eventually assumed that Stephen had been murdered. His wife was pregnant at the time and gave birth to a son three months after Stephen's disappearance.

By dropping "Bross," he changed his name to simply Stephen Decatur and joined the U.S. Army. He marched under General Kearney to Santa Fe then south into Chihauhua, Mexico. Decatur was well remembered by Colonel Clay Taylor as a brave soldier. After the Mexican War ended, Decatur operated a ferry boat near Council Bluffs, Iowa and also ran a shoe repair shop in the ferry house.

In Omaha, Nebraska, in 1857 or 1858, Stephen Decatur was recognized by a former pupil. Meanwhile, his brother had become Lieutenant Governor of the State of Illinois and worked for the Chicago Tribune. Lt. Governor William Bross was notified and immediately traveled to Omaha. William recognized Stephen at once. In a strange turn of events, Stephen denied any relationship and even threatened the life of the Lt. Governor.

While living in Nebraska, Decatur married again and became the father of three children. He also founded the town of Decatur. Gold fever seized Decatur in 1859, and he abandoned his second family in Nebraska to disappear once again.

Lt. Governor Bross, upon hearing this, traveled to Nebraska to console Stephen's second wife. He told her of Stephen's previous marriage and the pattern of abandoning his family. She had known nothing about this and was crushed by the news.

Decatur was counted among Colorado's pioneers and was a member of the Third Colorado Regiment. He participated in the infamous Sand Creek massacre under Col. Chivington. For a while, he prospected in the Peru Creek area of Summit County. The town of Decatur, formed near the Pennsylvania mine, was named for Stephen Decatur. He represented Summit County in the Territorial Legislature in 1867 and 1868.

In 1869, Stephen Decatur moved to Georgetown and began a career as associate editor of *The Colorado Miner*, a job he held for four years. He remained a man of mystery who flatly refused to divulge any of his past life. His nickname was "Old Sulphurets", but he was also known as "Commodore" Decatur.

Decatur was responsible for entering Colorado in the Industrial Exposition in Philadelphia with a display or ores from various Colorado mines. Eventually, the state awarded Decatur $1,000 for his help in advertising Colorado's mineral resources.

While in Georgetown, he developed an insatiable appetite for liquor and drank from early in the day until evening. This impoverished him and eventually Stephen Decatur drifted south to Custer County to work as Justice of the Peace. For a decade, he lived in what was termed "reduced circumstances." Eventually, the U.S. Government recognized his contribution during the Mexican War and granted him a pension. For the most part, he relied on the kindness of the residents of Rosita who provided him with a place to live and food. Decatur died alone in May, 1881, and he is buried in an unmarked grave in the Rosita Cemetery.

Stephen Decatur Bross was associate editor of The Colorado Miner *for four years, and during that time, refused to divulge any of his past life. He had good reason, since he abandoned his first wife and children to fight in the Mexican War and abandoned his second wife and children to come to Colorado. (Kenneth Jessen collection)*

GEORGETOWN BUSINESSES

George Clark and Jerome Chaffee were Georgetown's first bankers, but it wasn't long before William Cushman opened the Bank of Georgetown. In 1872, he contracted to have a commercial building constructed to house the bank. The Cushman Block was finished in 1875 with the completion of a third floor and remains standing today. Included in the structure was a full-size theater on the top floor with an excellent stage, room for a number of painted backdrops and even an orchestra pit. The theater was furnished with comfortable chairs and became very popular among Georgetown residents.

This was how the Cushman Block looked originally. It was built between 1872 and 1875 and became Georgetown's tallest building. For each floor the decorative lintels are different giving the structure a unique quality. (Denver Public Library, Western History Department F11148)

The theater was used from 1876 to 1882. In December 1879, there was a play, "Mary Stuart," starring Madame Janauschek. She was billed as the greatest living actress in the United States. According to a Leadville newspaper, the resounding applause during one of the performances was so great that it caused a serious structural crack in the balcony. From that point on in the play, the audience was asked to remain silent. To dispel any fears concerning this structure, a Georgetown committee had the building professionally inspected, and on January 10, 1880, the results were published. The building was found to be in perfectly safe condition.

After 1882, the theater closed, and the third floor was used by the Masons as their hall.

The Cushman Block as it appears today. It was the tallest building in Georgetown until its roof collapsed. The third floor had to be removed. (photograph by Kenneth Jessen)

As time passed, the structure deteriorated, and in 1969, a wet, heavy snow fell in Georgetown causing the collapse of the roof which fell into the then unoccupied third floor. At this point, the building's third floor had to be removed. After renovation during the early 1970s, the Cushman Block has been put back into use.

A year after the Bank of Georgetown opened its doors, the Bank of Clear Creek County was ready for business. Its owner, Charles Fish, purchased a piece of property, razed a livery stable which occupied the property, then erected a wooden building to serve as the bank. In 1887, a saloon fire next door bank broke out, and before the flames could be extinguished, the bank was destroyed. Fish replaced the original structure two years later with a brick building which remains standing today.

The nearest post office was initially at Empire City over the narrow Union Pass road. Empire City got its post office in 1861, and it wasn't until June, 1866, that a post office was opened in Georgetown. The post master's salary was all of a dollar a month at the time. In just two years, a telegraph line was extended up Clear Creek from Denver.

As expected for a mining town, Georgetown had a large number of hotels relative to its population. This included one built by Billy Barton in 1867 and named the Barton House. The building burned to the ground, but was soon rebuilt. As demand increased, Barton constructed an annex, and it became Georgetown's largest hotel with thirty rooms. A. B. Leggett opened a hotel in 1869 which became the Ennis House when Miss Kate Ennis took over its ownership. It was located at 5th and Taos streets and became the oldest operating hotel in town. There was also the Yates House, the American House, and as covered elsewhere in this book, the magnificent Hotel de Paris. The Hotel Dewey was able to handle twenty five guests and catered to both the traveler and permanent resident. Several small hotels were located on 6th Street, including The Albion and Webb's Hotel.

The Forbes Pharmacy was located on the lower floor of the Cushman Block. Mr. Forbes is standing to the right of the other two gentlemen. "Leis Dandelion" tonic is advertised over the entrance, and a plumbing company was located in the basement. (Denver Public Library, Western History Department F5139)

Georgetown had an amazing variety of commercial businesses including those associated with the mining industry such as assay offices, mining supplies, blacksmith shops and mills. Hardware stores were quite common, and the growing town supported several lumber mills. The hardware stores also carried hay, grain, coal and lumber. There were those who specialized in certain items such as a blacksmith who made ore buckets and a carpenter who made ladders for the mines. Supporting the construction trade were plumbers and carpenters. Disputes over mining claims were practically a way of life, and this supported a number of law offices.

This was Jacob Snetzer's tailor shop at Taos and 5th Street. Snetzer was well known in the Clear Creek Valley for his excellent, quality work. He charged $18 for a pair of pants and another $35 for a coat and vest. This building remains standing today, but the false-front has been removed. (Colorado Historic Society, F38142)

Georgetown was the trade center for the entire area and, at one time, the third largest settlement in Colorado Territory. The store of F. J. Wood including items such as stationary, books, periodicals, toys, dolls, sporting goods, jewelry, wall clocks, mantle clocks and a wide variety of watches. A. M. Hill carried school supplies in his store. He also had a soda fountain and served ice cream. His store must have been very popular among the school children.

The Hancock Brothers took over an existing store, built in 1868, and sold groceries and mining supplies. But not to be overlooked was J.A. Schauer's bakery on Alpine Street. He also offered ice cream and sodas. Schauer's Meat Market carried hanging half sides of beef plus a wide variety of other meat items. A slaughter house was located north of town. Medical treatment was something the average miner could not afford, and this supported several drug stores which carried all types of home remedies. Georgetown did, however, have several doctors.

The Kneisel and Anderson grocery and hardware store on Rose Street is the oldest, continuously operated business in Georgetown. The store

46

itself predates the building. Henry Kneisel purchased a bakery shop down the street and worked there for a decade before forming a partnership with Emil Anderson. Emil became Henry's son-in-law. The two moved to the present location in 1893, and in addition to groceries, they also ran a bakery. Four generations of this family have continued to operated this store.

The Bank of Clear Creek County was housed in this wood-frame building at Rose and 6th Street. Its owner, Charles Fish, purchased the property and razed a livery stable to make room for this structure. In 1887, a fire started in the saloon next door and destroyed the bank. Fish replaced the original structure with one made of brick which remains standing today. (Denver Public Library, Western History Department F5137)

Facing south onto 6th Street is the Fish Block. On this corner, the wood-frame Bank of Clear Creek County was built. Destroyed by fire in 1887, it was replaced by this brick structure. Fish sold the section on the left to the Masons. (photograph by Kenneth Jessen)

Kneisel & Anderson's general store was moved to this location in 1893 and became a popular 6th Street business. Their delivery wagon is pictured in front of what is Georgetown's oldest continuously operated business. (Denver Public Library, Western History Department F37779)

The John A. Morris Saloon occupied a typical false-front commercial building. Antlers were added over the side entrance and in the center of the false front. (Denver Public Library, Western History Department F5283)

This is an interior view of F. J. Wood's Book & Jewelry Store showing a wide variety of clocks and watches. (Denver Public Library, Western History Department F5177)

Charles Pollard operated this grocery store, which also carried hardware items as evidenced by the pots and pans in the window. (Denver Public Library, Western History Department F125)

This is Miss Burney's Millinery store in 1889. The four ladies in the front of the store are dressed in the finest fashions of the day. This store changed hands during the 1890s and became a laundry. (Denver Public Library, Western History Department F6789)

THE HOG PEN LYNCHING

Robert Schamle (spelled Schramle in some sources) raped a young girl in Sedalia, Missouri in 1877 and fled to the remote mining areas of Colorado in hopes of escaping prosecution. He settled in Georgetown and went to work for a respectable German butcher named Henry Thedie. The slaughter house was located about two miles below Georgetown. Henry Thedie lived near the slaughter house with his wife and three small children. On October 13, 1877, Thedie came to work with $80 in his wallet. Schamle shot and killed the German in cold blood for his money. Schamle used a borrowed gun he obtained the previous day. He was also spotted with the murder weapon after the killing.

Fortunately for Schamle, the butcher's body was not discovered until the following morning. This gave the murderer time to escape. Local law officers tried to solve the case, but they only had authority over the immediate area and had no means of tracking Schamle. After two weeks, the Rocky Mountain Detective Agency was called upon to help. Under the direction of General David Cook, detectives found that the killer's trail led to Pueblo.

Pat Desmond, deputized by Pueblo Sheriff Abe Ellis, hung around the cattle yard down by the tracks of the Denver & Rio Grande Railroad. He knew Schamle and knew his habits. Sure enough, Schamle wandered into the cattle yard where Pat Desmond was waiting. Desmond hesitated for a moment because of Schamle's casual attitude. The murderer didn't act at all guilty. This caught Desmond off guard, and in the blink of an eye, Schamle swung into a passing freight car.

Desmond returned to Sheriff Ellis and was told to chase Schamle. By simply following the railroad tracks, the killer was soon taken into custody. When Schamle found out that a man from Georgetown was on his way to make a positive identification, he remarked, "I wonder if they'll hang me?"

To save his neck, Schamle changed his plea from guilty to one of self-defense. In mid-December, he was taken to the Georgetown jail to wait trail. An ominous murmur could be heard on the normally quite streets of Georgetown. Law-abiding citizens took up arms, and one night, a group of masked men headed to the jail. The jailers were asleep, and at about four in the morning, they awoke to a crowd of masked men with guns.

Some of the men took the keys to the jail, while others covered the jailers. The keys were tossed back into the jailer's room, and the jailers quickly discovered that their prisoner was missing.

There are no accounts of what took place that night, but when morning came, Schamle's cold, partially clothed corpse was found swinging by the neck from the frame of a dilapidated building a few hundred feet from the Georgetown jail. The structure was used as a hog pen. The body remained until about nine in the morning when the coroner cut it down. It was then dumped into the box where the hogs slept and left for several more hours while Georgetown residents passed by.

The vigilantes were regarded as public benefactors. Georgetown residents showed little remorse over the actions of its citizens which were even applauded by the town's Presbyterian minister. Edward Wolcott, a Georgetown lawyer who would eventually become a U.S. Senator, wrote his parents that he would gladly prosecute the lynch mob, but that no Colorado Grand Jury would convict them.

This engraving depicts the hanging of Robert Schamle over a hog pen for the murder of a German butcher. (Kenneth Jessen collection)

A FRAGMENT OF OLD FRANCE

Adolphe Francois Gerard was born in France in 1844 and was initially enrolled in seminary. This apparently did not agree with him, and he switched to the study of culinary art. Eventually, he felt there was more opportunity in the United States and arrived in New York City in 1866. According to some accounts, he sold articles to *Frank Leslie's Illustrated Newspaper* and was promptly accused of plagiarism. Adolphe then joined the U.S. Army in Brooklyn, New York in 1868, and the following year, deserted. This forced him to change his name and to vanish in the vast American West. From this time on, he called himself Louis Dupuy.

In Denver, he began working for *The Rocky Mountain News* as a carrier or a reporter, depending on the source. Whatever the case, he ended up as a miner in Georgetown. In 1873, while working in the Kennedy mine, he and another miner fired off two shots of dynamite. They entered the mine only to discover that one of the shots failed to fire due to a defective, slow-burning fuse. The delayed shot exploded while Dupuy was in the mine, and he was badly injured.

After recovering in the Georgetown hospital, he realized that he could not continue mining and rented the Delmonico's Bakery on Alpine Street. He made the place into a first class restaurant serving oysters, wild game and other delicacies. He purchased the bakery plus two other adjacent buildings and began work on a hotel. Dupuy did most of the work on his French Provincial hotel which he named The Hotel de Paris.

The Hotel de Paris was built in phases with the first part of the work completed in the 1870s. The three buildings were eventually joined in the 1890s by a single masonry facade to form a single, massive-looking structure. From the rear, however, it is still apparent, due to the variations in the window style, that the Hotel de Paris is three separate structures. The masonry walls are three feet thick and covered with stucco. Painted square outlines on the stucco give the external appearance of cut blocks of stone.

On the first floor were a half dozen rooms including the dining room, library, kitchen and Dupuy's own living quarters. There was also a courtyard behind the structure surrounded by a high wall. On the second floor were ten guest bedrooms complete with modern conveniences such as running water and electricity. The Hotel de Paris was completed in 1890.

An interesting omission for a frontier hotel was the bar. Dupuy served only the finest French wines instead. He ordered entire casks and did his own bottling. At least twenty-eight of the greatest labels in France were represented on his wine shelves. The wine was stored in a cellar which also included a cold storage room for meat.

The dining room in the Hotel de Paris was Dupuy's showplace, with a floor consisting of alternating strips of walnut and maple. Walnut was also used for the wainscoting which extended around the walls. Even the stippled plaster applied to the ceilings and walls was extra fancy. A decorative quarter-inch rope was glued to the walls and painted over to create a panel-like effect.

Louis Dupuy was the name he was known by in Georgetown, but his real name was Adolphe Francois Gerard. He was born in France arriving in New York City in 1866. After a year in the Army, he deserted and fled to Georgetown to build one of Colorado's finest hotels, The Hotel de Paris. (Colorado Historical Society F128)

The hotel had its own indoor fountain stocked with live trout. This was a convenient means to keep the trout fresh, and there was also a tank for live lobsters. Dupuy served fresh oysters, Porterhouse steak, sirloin steak, veal cutlet, mutton chops, fried mackerel, fried tripe, apple fritters, welsh rarebit and a variety of other dishes.

Most of Dupuy's magic was created in his kitchen. Shining copper pots and pans hung ready to use from hooks on one wall. A centrally located six foot by eight foot oven was used for the baking. The kitchen also had a skylight and two sinks.

Louis Dupuy was well-read and had an extensive collection of fine books in his private library. Books both in French, German and English could be found on a wide variety of subjects.

As for his personality, Louis was gruff at times, while at other times he could be quite hospitable and gracious. He was known for turning away undesirable guests and even sending them to another hotel. Because they were steady and repeat customers, Louis liked traveling salesmen. Dupuy hated crowds and at one time, closed the Hotel de Paris on the Fourth of July just to avoid the mass of humanity which roamed the streets.

Louis Dupuy fell in love with a young Georgetown girl who rejected him. He wrote her many romantic letters telling of his deep love. The letters were to no avail, and she married another man leaving Dupuy heartbroken. After she left Georgetown, some accounts say he began to hate women.

Dupuy believed man to be a machine and work to be the output of stored energy. He also believed that man had to work to prevent "rusting." He told much of this to the noted Dean of Columbia's Teachers College, Dr. James Russell. Dupuy believed that certain foods provided the human body a better foundation for life and work. During a visit to the Hotel de Paris by Dr. Russell, Dupuy at first treated him with skepticism and disdain. Dupuy pressed Russell, asking him what kind of man he was intellectually. Once Dupuy discovered that Russell was well-educated and a thinker, the two talked until three the following morning ignoring fatigue. Russell was introduced to the notion that cooking was a science and that mankind's survival depended on the quality of food consumed. From this, Russell got the idea that domestic science should be taught in school. Of Dupuy, Russell said that he was no crude thinker and was well versed in different types of philosophy. Dupuy knew how the digestive system worked and the importance of a proper diet.

There were no servants in the Hotel de Paris, however, there was "Aunt" Sophie Gally. She was French, and Dupuy referred to her as a guest, yet she waited tables and made the beds. Sophie was a tiny woman who pulled her hair back tightly over her head, then tied it in a knot in the back. Sophie commonly wore a white apron over a black dress and spoke little English. She rarely left the hotel. Louis provided her with a room and an allowance of twenty dollars a month.

Dupuy's morning ritual was to take a bath in ice-cold mountain water. These cold baths possibly led to his contracting pneumonia in September, 1900. Dupuy died soon after leaving his estate to Sophie Gally. Both he and Sophie had made out identical wills leaving their respective estates to one another. After Louis passed away, Sophie had her will changed to leave her estate to distant relatives in France. The following year, she followed Louis Dupuy in death.

The Hotel de Paris was built by Frenchman Louis DuPuy who started out by turning a bakery into a first class restaurant. Its masonry walls are three feet thick and covered with stucco. Painted square outlines on the stucco give the external appearance of stone. (photograph by Kenneth Jessen)

A PHILOSOPHIC REPAIR SHOP

Georgetown had its share of characters, and possibly the most eccentric was Benjamin Franklin Southgate. He constructed a home at the base of Chimney Rock. This rock has its own history and once supported a high chimney for the Georgetown Silver Company's smelter. A long brick flue was laid up the side of the rock to connect the furnace inside the smelter with the chimney creating an arrangement totally unique in Colorado mining towns.

When Southgate came to Georgetown to live, he was already in his seventies. He kept busy at many different trades. Above the door to his shop he had the following, thought provoking description of his business, "1900, Franklin Hermatage <sic>, Philosophic Scientific Repair Shop, Clocks, Coppering Chairs, Saws Filed, Tinware, Politicks <sic> and Theology Tinkerd."

He renamed Chimney Rock "Bunker Hill" and built a flight of wooden stairs up one side. At the top, he blasted out a tomb where he wanted to be buried. He also constructed a wooden monument next to the tomb on which he carved the cryptic message "The End of the Road to Eternity." A local Georgetown ordinance prohibited a burial within the city limits, and Southgate ended up with other departed residents in the Alvarado Cemetery. The monument was moved to adorn the head of his grave.

In his front yard, he had a water powered merry-go-round. Children flocked to his yard and paid a nickel for a ride. In the process, the children would get to hear about all of Ben's many experiences. As if the merry-go-round were not entertaining enough, inside Southgate's workshop were a variety of water powered toys.

Southgate left behind many fond memories, especially among Georgetown's children.

Here is Southgate's "Philosophic Repair Shop" located at the base of Chimney Rock. Careful examination of this photograph shows nine children riding the water-powered merry-go-round in his front yard. (Colorado Historical Society F15270)

SOILED DOVES

Not generally discussed in polite company nor covered in local newspapers were the prostitutes. This was especially true in Georgetown, which was attempting to become more refined than the average Colorado mining town. Prostitution, however, was considered a necessity of life in a mining town where men outnumbered women by an enormous ratio. Only a man wishing to remain chaste might not be tempted at one time or another by the soiled doves. On Georgetown's west side, across Clear Creek, were five houses of ill repute. Most of the stories of these ladies of the evening are filled with sorrow.

A good-looking seventeen-year-old girl arrived in Georgetown by train in 1877. She was well-educated and apparently possessed some degree of refinement. She voluntarily became one of Madam Lottee White's girls, and among the miners she was known as "Tid-bit."

After two weeks, a lady of obvious breeding arrived on the daily train from Denver. Immediately, she went to the police looking for her younger sister. She explained that her sister married an abusive husband, was driven from home and fled to Denver. The girl then went to Idaho Springs and finally Georgetown. From the lady's description of her sister, it was easy for the police to make the connection with the prostitute Tid-bit.

When Tid-bit saw her older sister, she was overcome with joy that someone in her family had cared enough to rescue her from a life of shame. The two sisters left town on the afternoon train never to be seen again, at least not on the streets of Georgetown.

The local law was clear on prostitution; it was illegal. The pioneer parlor-house madam of Georgetown was Mattie Estes. Her real name was Elizabeth C. Dyo. Apparently parlor houses were allowed to operate as long as they did not disturb the peace. For some reason, Mattie Estes was singled out and hauled into court. The official charge was keeping a "bawdy house." In the trial which followed, a jury found her guilty, despite the fact that the defense had pointed our that Mattie Estes had a license. It was a license to sell wine, however, and nothing else!

In 1884, at the age of 60, Mattie Estes passed away. She had traveled to New Orleans for her health. At the time of her death, she was said to be quite wealthy as a result of "...her disreputable vocation." She left her fortune to her man, King.

The story of Lizzie Greer was truly tragic. She was very attractive and began work as a factory girl on the East Coast. Her employer made sexual advances toward her, and for one reason or another, she was provided a one-way ticket west. In Georgetown, she became the live-in mistress of Sam Wade. Another miner named Hayes took a strong interest in Lizzie. Sam became insanely jealous and killed Hayes.

Sam Wade made the mistake of returning to the scene of the crime the morning following the murder only to be surrounded by two law officers. He called for Lizzie, his mistress, and used her as a shield. He held the girl with one arm and pointed a pistol at her head with his free hand. The officers held their ground and waited. Wade suddenly released the girl and fled up the hillside above his mine. He was felled by a single bullet and was buried at Mill City (Dumont) in the same grave as his victim, Hayes.

Years later, Lizzie Greer was found dead in a coal shed near the Windsor Hotel in lower downtown Denver. She had been working as a prostitute and was only twenty years old at the time.

Ada La Monte was, in some way, involved in a murder. Her real name was Ellen A. Mohier, and she was born in Rochester, New York. She began her career as a bareback rider in a circus. By the age of seventeen, she was a practicing prostitute. She arrived in Georgetown to continue her profession in 1860, making her one of Georgetown's pioneers. She married and became "an honest woman."

In 1873, three Chinese women moved into a house near Clear Creek in Georgetown for what the newspaper referred to as "...ways that are dark and tricks that are vain." They were reputed to be willing to entertain a dozen or more men per night, a far greater number than the worst of the prostitutes on Georgetown's "row." They were referred to as "...these three almond-eyed daughters of the Orient." They also ran a laundry business on the side.

Eventually, Georgetown eliminated all of its prostitutes and became a fully respectable town.

PICTURESQUE GEORGETOWN

Thanks in part to an excellent volunteer fire department during its early years, a good number of nineteenth century structures are left to see. Other mining towns suffered devastating fires which virtually wiped out their older, wood-frame buildings. Georgetown did have its serious fires, but none which burned the entire town. These photographs represent just a sample of the wonderful buildings which make Georgetown a special place to visit.

This is one of Georgetown's fine nineteenth century homes. Located at 4th and Argentine, this lavishly furnished mansion was built by Thomas Cornish and later owned by Frank Graham. Graham owned one of the rich silver mines in the area and was killed by a falling rock while working in his mine. (photograph by Kenneth Jessen)

John Bowman and his family arrived in Georgetown during the 1880s, a time of great prosperity. Bowman was successful in his silver mining ventures and built this beautiful home in 1892. One of their daughters inherited the house and married John White. The Bowman-White house remained in the family until its purchase in 1974 by Historic Georgetown Inc. (photograph by Kenneth Jessen)

Historic Georgetown Inc. did not want to leave the impression that their collection of homes represented only the wealthy. The Tucker-Rutherford House typifies how the typical miner or mill worker might have lived. The Tucker brothers, Georgetown merchants, constructed the front two rooms during the 1870s or 1880s, then they added a shed roof back bedroom in the 1890s to complete the house. (photograph by Kenneth Jessen)

This striking Gothic Revival home, with its steep roof and nicely appointed bay window, was the home of John Adams Church. It was designed by architect Robert Roeschlaub and was constructed during 1876-1877 for Church, who made his living speculating with ore processing methods. (photograph by Kenneth Jessen)

This is the back door of the second McClellan Hall restored for local melodramas in 1946. The front of this building faces the central business district, but will not last long at the present rate of deterioration. Some of the brick used during this time came from a Georgetown brick kiln and was of inferior quality. (photograph by Kenneth Jessen)

This old stone jail was built in 1883 by the town of Georgetown to house less violent criminals. This old jail sits by itself along Argentine Street near the central business district and is now owned by the county. (photograph by Kenneth Jessen)

The Grace Episcopal Church, located on the east side of Taos Street, was built in 1869-70. The pipe organ was installed in 1877 and is still in operating order. The bell tower to call the faithful to church is detached and located on the opposite side of the church. (photograph by Kenneth Jessen)

This beautiful brick home once sat along the wagon road between Georgetown and Silver Plume on the north side of Clear Creek. It was built by Henry Crow, then sold to Julius Pohle, a German chemist who became manager of the Lebanon Mining Company. When I-70 was surveyed, the Pohle House sat in the direct path of the interstate and was moved. Today, it is owned by the State Historical Society with plans for its restoration. (photograph by Kenneth Jessen)

The Community Center at 6th Street and Argentine was built in 1868 to house the Ohio Bakery. When Georgetown became the county seat, Clear Creek County rented this building, then purchased it to served as the courthouse, complete with rocking chairs for the jury. After over a century of use, a new courthouse was built. (photograph by Kenneth Jessen)

The Maxwell House on 4th Street has been rated as one of the ten outstanding examples of Victorian architecture in the United States. It was originally constructed by a Georgetown storekeeper named Potter and began as a modest two-story home. When Potter struck it rich, he put on an addition in the front which eclipsed the original structure. Mining engineer Frank Maxwell purchased the house from Potter and lived in it for fifty years. (photograph by Kenneth Jessen)

The exact age of this cabin is unknown, and it may pre-date mining in the Georgetown area, therefore, the town itself. Cabins like this were the first structures in the valley, but as Georgetown grew in size and wealth, they were replaced by substantial homes and businesses made of brick or milled lumber. This cabin once sat at the foot of Democrat Mountain, in the path of I-70, and was moved to a safe location. It is owned by Historic Georgetown Inc. (photograph by Kenneth Jessen)

Facing 3rd Street below the Guanella Pass road, this structure is the Centennial Reduction Works. It was built around the turn of the century and most likely was used to process zinc ore. It is the only remaining mill in Georgetown. This view is of the mill's back entrance. (photograph by Kenneth Jessen)

This is one of the few log structures left in Georgetown. Log structures were quickly replaced by ones constructed of milled lumber once the saw mills were able to meet demand. This structure is located at the north end of Argentine Street and was once a mining company office. (photograph by Kenneth Jessen)

THE FAMOUS GEORGETOWN LOOP

The Colorado Central, with its headquarters in Golden, constructed a standard gauge railroad to Denver and north through Fort Collins to Cheyenne. It also built a narrow gauge railroad up Clear Creek Canyon to serve the mining industry at Black Hawk. The railroad's management realized it could generate even more revenue if it included Idaho Springs and Georgetown. The Colorado Central installed a switch at Forks Creek with one branch going up the North Fork of Clear Creek to Black Hawk and the other branch going up the South Fork to Georgetown.

The Georgetown branch was completed in August, 1877, and a depot was constructed near 11th and Rose streets. The large depot measured twenty-five feet by one hundred and one feet and is used today by the Georgetown Loop Railroad as a gift shop and cafe. At one time, there were also stockyards, a section house, and a water tank.

The Union Pacific had been financing much of the construction and eventually gained control over the Colorado Central. Several years after reaching Georgetown, the Colorado Central made plans to build to Silver Plume and beyond. This extension was so costly that for it to merely serve the mines in upper Clear Creek was clearly impractical. The work was part of a much bigger scheme.

During the time the Colorado Central was grading and laying track up Clear Creek, the narrow gauge Denver, South Park & Pacific was building southwest through Waterton, up the Platte River Canyon, over Kenosha Pass and west across South Park through Fairplay to Buena Vista. Another narrow gauge railroad, the Denver & Rio Grande, constructed a line through the Royal Gorge to Salida then north to Leadville. It was first to capture the lucrative Leadville traffic.

Narrow gauge was selected for various reasons. In Colorado, narrow gauge meant three feet between the rails instead of four feet, eight and a half inches. This greatly reduced the width of the grade, therefore, its cost. Most important, it allowed for much sharper curves, and the use of smaller, less expensive locomotives and cars.

Jay Gould, of the Union Pacific, entered the railroad picture in Colorado. He knew the Union Pacific had to develop a feeder system for its main transcontinental line and share the ever increasing mine traffic in Colorado to be successful. Such traffic was ideally suited for a railroad with coal, supplies and heavy equipment going to the mines. Coming from the mines were ore, bullion and concentrate. Gould convinced the owners of the Denver, South Park & Pacific to sell to the Union Pacific at a handsome profit for its original investors. Now Gould was positioned to try two approaches to reach Leadville and take away the Rio Grande's business. One route involved extending the Denver, South Park & Pacific from Como north over Boreas Pass, down into Breckenridge, then over Fremont Pass. The other route was an extension of the Colorado Central beyond Georgetown, over Loveland Pass and down to Keystone where it was to join the Denver, South Park & Pacific. Instead, only the Denver, South Park & Pacific reached Leadville; the Colorado Central failed to extend its service more than a few miles beyond Silver Plume.

A double-header is shown crossing the Devil's Gate Viaduct pulling just seven cars in May, 1938, the last year of operation. The train is headed to Silver Plume. This fine photograph was taken by one of Colorado's greatest photographers, Dick Kindig. (Dick Kindig, Kenneth Jessen collection)

Typical of other Union Pacific projects, a subsidiary was incorporated under the name of the Georgetown, Breckenridge & Leadville to take the Colorado Central from its terminus in Georgetown across the Continental

Divide to Keystone. In 1879, a corps of surveyors, under the direction of Edward Berthoud, began work. There were two primary physical obstacles: Loveland Pass, which would require a long tunnel, and the steep rise in a narrow canyon from Georgetown to Silver Plume.

Union Pacific location engineer Robert Blickensderfer was given the task of finding a route to Silver Plume. In the first two miles beyond Georgetown, the canyon gained 638 feet. To simply follow Clear Creek would have resulted in 6% grades, far beyond the capability of an adhesion railroad. To overcome this steep section, Blickensderfer had to find a way to lengthen the line within the confines of the narrow valley. He used a complete spiral where the track crossed over itself, plus two loops to reverse direction. The track was stretched out to nearly four and a half miles, and the grade was cut to 3 1/2%. This piece of railroad engineering resulted in one of the most spectacular rides in Colorado and became known as the Georgetown Loop. From Silver Plume, the line was extended an additional four miles.

Grading was done beyond Georgetown at a slow pace, and by the end of 1881, only a half mile of grade was ready for rail. A great deal of energy was spent surveying the line over Loveland Pass and down to Keystone. Bids for grading were opened by the Union Pacific, and the contract for the grade beyond Georgetown was awarded. All at once, two hundred men were at work. The stonework for the bridges on the Georgetown Loop was done during the middle of 1883. The track layers came in August, and the smaller bridges were put into place. Track layers, beginning at a point below Georgetown, reached the abutment for the high bridge or Devil's Gate Viaduct in September.

In order for the railroad to climb at a constant rate to reach a point above the Devil's Gate, the grade had to begin below Georgetown. The grade ran above most of the town on the east side and crossed the Guanella Pass road. This put the Georgetown depot on a spur track and not on the main line. Trains entering Georgetown had to depart by backing out to the switch below town.

Construction of the high bridge was fraught with many problems. It was fabricated by a Pennsylvania company. They were also contracted to erect the structure. It was officially installed and ready for rail on November 25, 1883, but the Union Pacific's chief engineer refused to accept it as complete. The riveting was defective and the columns had been placed in the wrong order. The columns at the north end should have been placed on the south end and vice versa. The structure had to be dismantled and erected properly. The work was completed by January 23, 1884, to the satisfaction of the Union Pacific.

Track laying across the high bridge took place immediately, but due to bad weather, the first locomotive did not venture across until the first of March. The bridge proved sturdy and served the railroad for over fifty years. Some additional bracing was added, however, in 1921. The first train chugged into Silver Plume on March 11, and the final four miles to Graymont was completed in mid-April. The entire cost of the project was a little over a quarter of a million dollars.

The bridge itself was a complex structure because it was part of a complete spiral. It was built on an eighteen degree curve and had a 3 1/2% grade. The upper level of track was seventy-five feet above the lower level of track and nearly one hundred feet above Clear Creek. Above the Devil's Gate Viaduct, the line paralleled Clear Creek then doubled back on itself using a loop crossing Clear Creek twice within a relatively short distance. At the top of a tangent, the railroad went around a second loop called the High Fill on a curve with a radius of only 193 feet. A standard gauge railroad could not have been built using such sharp curves. After several less spectacular curves, the tracks reached Silver Plume. In less than three miles, the railroad twisted through 3 1/2 complete circles.

The railroad sensed the importance of tourist traffic and took full advantage of the Georgetown Loop. A series of promotional panoramic photographs were taken with four trains posed at different points along the loop. A pavilion was constructed near the Silver Plume depot along with a tall, rustic clock. Visitors to Silver Plume could ride the Sunrise Peak Aerial "Railway" or bucket tram. The Argentine Central, built in 1905-1906, originated from Silver Plume and offered excursions to a point near the top of McClellan Mountain, above 13,000 feet, using a series of switchbacks.

From Denver, Leadville was 276 miles via the Rio Grande and 171 via the Denver, South Park & Pacific through Buena Vista. When the Boreas Pass route was complete, the mileage to Leadville via the South Park was cut to 151. Had the line over the Georgetown Loop been completed, the distance from Denver to Leadville would have been 127 miles. A 3,000 foot tunnel under Loveland Pass would have been required, however. Some construction was done on this tunnel, but when the magnitude of this work sank into the minds of Union Pacific management, drilling was stopped.

In 1893, after the repeal of the Sherman Silver Purchase Act, silver mining began to decline, and with it, the need for railroad service. In the meantime, the Union Pacific had gone bankrupt and the narrow gauge line to Georgetown was taken over by the Colorado & Southern. Beginning in 1917, the line began to lose money despite its good tourist business, so service was cut back. The losses continued to mount, and the Colorado & Southern management realized that if the remainder of its railroad were to survive, the narrow gauge portion would have to be abandoned. Maintenance all but came to a halt, and in 1931, the railroad petitioned to abandon the line from Black Hawk to Central City. This was just the beginning, and in 1936, the railroad petitioned to abandon the entire line from Golden to Silver Plume and from Forks Creek to Black Hawk, a total of 46 miles.

Service tapered off to three times a week then dwindled to twice a week. Because of an upswing in mining activity, the Interstate Commerce Commission required the Colorado & Southern to continue to operate for another three years. During 1937, business picked up and tri-weekly service was resumed. During this time, deflation of the dollar helped keep costs down.

Abandonment, however, was inevitable. On January 30, 1939, the last revenue train ran up the South Fork of Clear Creek as far as Empire Junction, several miles below Georgetown. Dismantling began immediately. All of the rail was pulled up by March 21 from Idaho Springs to Silver Plume, and the famed Georgetown Loop passed into history. The Devil's Gate Viaduct was sold to a mining company for $450 and was removed in the spring to be used for mine supports. The rails netted a few dollars in scrap metal. The portion of the line from Golden to Idaho Springs was taken up the following year. Ore was hauled from the mines in Clear Creek County to the mills in Leadville by truck, a trip which took seven or eight hours over Loveland Pass. In contrast, the 317 mile trip over the narrow gauge railroad system via Denver through South Park required five to six days. With the Colorado & Southern out of the way, it was possible to construct a modern paved highway up to the mountain towns in Gilpin and Clear Creek Counties using, for the most part, the abandoned right-of-way.

Many of Georgetown's commercial structures were abandoned by the end of World War II as shown in this 1946 photograph of the Monti and Guanella Block. Although modified, this building still stands and is Georgetown's oldest surviving business building. It was constructed in 1867. (Denver Public Library, Western History Department F10902)

Projects like this, where the Lebanon mine and its buildings were reconstructed, attract tourists. During the summer, a ticket to take a guided tour of the Lebanon mine can be purchased as part of the ride on the Georgetown Loop. (photograph by Kenneth Jessen)

GEORGETOWN'S DECLINE

All Colorado mining towns have suffered some form of decline during their history. A few have been abandoned and repopulated as many as three times; most towns were abandoned entirely. The demand for coal, uranium, silver, gold or molybdenum has fluctuated, and underground wealth is not renewable. Mines reached depths where the cost of ore extraction exceeded its value. Georgetown depended on the price of silver which was, in part, artificially maintained by the U. S. Government.

Dating back to 1792, the United States adopted both gold and silver as common currency. This created a market for both metals, but mill owners could also sell these metals on the open market. In the early 1800s, the U.S. Government undervalued silver. The result was that individuals melted down their silver coins which had a face value less than the silver content on the open market. Silver was driven out of the currency in favor of gold. During the Civil War, however, the government issued paper currency called "greenbacks" with no coinage to back it. Lack of precious metal to back the currency produced high inflation which forced a return to a metallic standard.

Colorado produced so much silver that over-production caught up with the demand dropping the price of silver on the open market. In 1873, the U.S. Government demonetized silver, but in 1878, the Bland-Allison Act brought a limited amount back into circulation, which meant that the U. S. Treasury was obligated to purchase some silver. The depressed price of silver forced some mines to close, and Georgetown's population, which once stood at 5,000, began to drop. Mine owners, whose income once depended solely on silver production, began to diversify their investments.

The silver producing states reacted by pushing Congress for a bimetallic currency with free and unlimited coinage of silver at a sixteen to one ratio with gold. This would have assured Georgetown miners a market for their silver.

The Sherman Silver Purchase Act was passed in 1890 and required the purchase of even more silver than the Bland-Allison Act. Prices rose, then fell to sixty-two cents per ounce by July, 1893. The Treasury, however, was forced to use some of its gold reserves for the purchase of silver. Most of the profits from silver production seemed to end up in the pockets of wealthy mine owners. The purchase of silver also favored only a few western states. President Cleveland called a special session of Congress to discuss the silver problem and to repeal the Sherman Act. For fourteen days, Colorado Senators Teller and Wolcott used a filibuster to keep up a valiant, non-stop debate over the issue without a recess.

The senators finally gave up, and both the Senate and House voted to repeal the Sherman Silver Purchase Act in August, 1893. The price of silver plummeted to less than forty cents relative to its previous high of over a dollar an ounce. This made most silver mining operations uneconomical. By this time, many mines were at a depth where flooding was a problem and pumping was constant. Labor rates were also rising making mining less profitable.

The year 1893 marked the end of the boom years for Clear Creek County, and hundreds, then thousands of men were put out of work in the mines and the mills. Most mines never reopened even after the price of silver made a modest recovery. Georgetown's resident population fell to several hundred with over half the town abandoned. Individuals trying to sell their homes and businesses found little market for the property. Georgetown, however, could look back on over three decades of prosperity, longer than most other mining towns. Its success, however, was bolstered not by the intrinsic value of what was mined, but rather by the artificial demand for silver created by politicians.

During the early part of the twentieth century, limited mining continued in the Georgetown area as new metals were discovered. For a while, zinc was in demand, and World War I increased the need for copper and lead. After the end of the war, prices for these metals fell. During World War II, scrap metal drives targeted the rusting, idle machinery in the mills. Most of this machinery was hauled off and melted down for the war effort.

Revitalization would come from tourism for communities like Georgetown. After slumbering for many decades, Georgetown woke to skier traffic, then to the creation of the Georgetown-Silver Plume Historic District. The Georgetown Loop Railroad over the Devil's Gate Viaduct was completed and opened to tourists in 1984. The Lebanon mine complex was restored and added to this attraction. Historic Georgetown Inc. operates the Hamill House for tours and has plans to restore other homes representative of the mining era. The Hotel de Paris is also open to the public and is run by the Colonial Dames. It now looks as though Georgetown is on sound footing.

RESTORATION OF THE GEORGETOWN LOOP

March 18, 1939, when the last rails were pulled up from the Georgetown Loop, was a sad day for many railroad historians. However, the idea of restoring this remarkable engineering feat was kept alive. Under the leadership of James Grafton Rogers, the Colorado Historical Society selected the valley between Georgetown and Silver Plume as the future site of an interpretive exhibit of early mining history. By the 1950s, precious metal mining had dwindled to a handful of mines leaving in its wake a trail of ghost towns, abandoned buildings, the remains of many mills and a collection of rusting machinery.

The area had the elements needed for the accurate reconstruction of Colorado's mining industry. As a bonus, had first been a gold mining region followed by a silver boom. Some of the mines were still intact, and some of the equipment was still in place. The old grade of the Colorado & Southern was still there, although eroded and overgrown. One of the abutments of the Devil's Gate Viaduct was missing completely, and the other was crumbling.

What could have destroyed this vision was the construction of I-70. Through careful planning and cooperation, additional money was appropriated to route the highway into the north wall of Republican Mountain. In the process, a minimum amount of damage was done to historic Georgetown, the mines and the railroad grade.

The State of Colorado was able to purchase or lease most of the land in the valley, thus saving it from commercial development. In 1966, the Union Pacific Railroad Foundation donated a modest $10,000 to get the restoration project started. The Silver Plume depot stood in the way of I-70, and the Loveland Ski Association moved this structure to a new site. The Lebanon Mine manager's house was also on the right-of-way and was moved by the highway contractor, the Lowdermilk Company. Colorado State University got its students involved in the identification of old mining sites. To reopen the Lebanon mine, the Climax Molybdenum Company offered its financial support.

In the summer of 1972, actual construction on the railroad began by the U.S. Army. An infantry division and elements of two engineering battalions were involved. The very first construction was a chain link fence around the Silver Plume depot area. Work on a new foundation for the depot was started. A Seabee unit was looking for actual work experience in building a railroad, and by luck, one needed to be built. Actual track laying was dubbed "Operation Silver Spike," and work started in 1973. Donated standard gauge ties were cut from eight feet down to six feet for use with the narrow gauge track.

The Seabees and U.S. Army worked on laying track up toward the Silver Plume yard. Before this track was connected to the yard tracks, a "speeder" was used to transport people. This speeder, however, needed a little push to get it up the steep 3 1/2% grade. (photograph by Kenneth Jessen)

A suitable sixty foot pin truss bridge was located in the Greeley area on the Colorado & Southern's abandoned Black Hollow Branch. It was trucked into a staging area above Georgetown and partially dismantled and painted. It was then moved into position to become the first major bridge replacement on the loop across Clear Creek. From its abandoned Boulder branch, the Union Pacific donated seventy-pound rail similar to the rail used on the loop during its final years of operation.

The second bridge over Clear Creek below Silver Plume was a fifty foot plate girder bridge. It once served as the turntable at Silver Plume from 1884 until it replaced the original, wooden Howe truss which had burned. At the time, the Colorado & Southern had built a wye at Silver Plume to allow the locomotives to be turned thus eliminating the need for a turntable. When the original Georgetown to Silver Plume line was dismantled, the bridge was sold or given away. It was believed that it ended up as a county road bridge near Fort Logan. The bridge, consisting of two girders, was recovered and transported to the staging area above Georgetown, repaired and painted. There were those who doubted that this was the same bridge once used on the Georgetown Loop, but when it dropped into the pockets in the concrete abutments perfectly, all doubt was eliminated.

The very first train to go down the reconstructed Georgetown Loop was on July 27, 1974, powered by a diesel-electric locomotive. It was used to haul two gondolas loaded with ballast to begin the long process of distributing ballast along the newly laid track. (photograph by Kenneth Jessen)

The U.S. Army worked at stabilizing the steep slope and deep cut adjacent to the pin truss. The cut itself was "V" in shape and was lined with hand-fitted rock. The locomotives to be used on the loop were substantially larger than the original steam engines and would not clear the sides of the cut. For that reason, the floor of the cut had to be elevated.

A Seabee camp was established in 1974 on a flat area which was once part of U.S. 6. Track laying progressed uphill toward the Silver Plume yards starting at the pin truss. In the meantime, a fifty ton, narrow gauge diesel-electric locomotive arrived.

After yard track at the Silver Plume depot was joined on July 27, 1974, with the rails extending down grade to the pin truss, a locomotive could be used to haul construction material and ballast. The first steam locomotive, No. 44, was transported from Central City where concessionaire Lindsey Ashby operated it over a portion of the Colorado Central grade below Central City. The locomotive, an outside frame 2-8-0 Baldwin built in 1921, was originally built for the International Railways of

Central America in El Salvador. It first operated on the reconstructed Georgetown Loop on August 24, 1974, to haul three fright cars and a caboose.

From time to time, special trains run on the Georgetown Loop as evidenced by this photographer's special which ran on June 22, 1975. The train is pulled by No. 44 and is on the rock wall just below Silver Plume. (photograph by Kenneth Jessen)

The Seabees and the U.S. Army got the project off to a good start. They replaced the major bridges down to the Devil's Gate Viaduct including a short wooden truss over the Hall Mine, and they laid 6,600 feet of track from the pin truss up to the Silver Plume yards. When they left, Lindsey Ashby and his people took over the responsibility of laying track from the pin truss down to the Devil's Gate Viaduct abutments. For a while, track laying proceeded without the benefit of an air compressor, and spikes had to be driven the old fashioned way, with a spike mall. Along with a handful of volunteers, Lindsey and his crew learned the art of being Gandy Dancers and could triple team a spike. Three men would swing at precisely different times, hitting the same spike in rapid succession. Rail and ties were also brought down on work trains and unloaded by hand.

On a typical railroad, ballast consists of crushed rock. In the Georgetown area, crushed rock was simply not available. The State of Colorado offered a mixture of sand and gravel from one of its gravel pits. When it dried, this mixture set like concrete. Several former Denver & Rio Grande bottom dump gondolas were loaded and brought down grade. When the doors on the gondolas were opened at a location requiring ballast, almost nothing fell out. It was clear that from then on, the ballast had to be hand shoveled out and hand distributed along the line. Tamping under the ties also was done by hand.

The end of track in early July, 1975, was just beyond the pin truss in a rock lined cut just below I-70. At this time, work on the second bridge over Clear Creek, the turntable bridge, had begun. (photograph by Kenneth Jessen)

Just days after work trains began to run, the railroad experienced its first derailment. The equipment used was very old and cast off by the Denver & Rio Grande. A kingpin on one of the trucks on a flat car was missing. When the car went around the first curve, which happened to be on the top of a narrow rock wall visible from I-70 just below Silver Plume, the car derailed. It took more than an hour to jack the car up and put it back on the track due to the lack of room on either side.

Working conditions at 9,000 feet were also difficult. Shortness of breath was one problem, but cold, hard rain storms in the afternoons

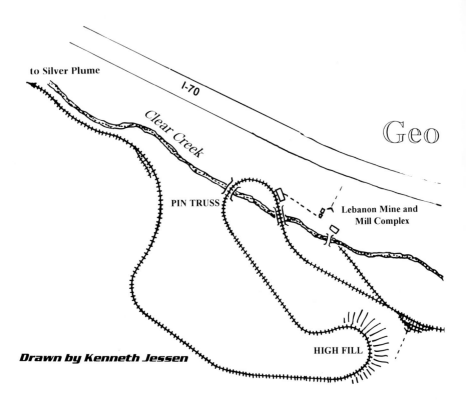

to Silver Plume

I-70

Clear Creek

Geo

PIN TRUSS

Lebanon Mine and
Mill Complex

HIGH FILL

Drawn by Kenneth Jessen

would force a temporary halt to the work. Due to short summer seasons, work was restricted to the warmer months, and the project remained idle for half a year at a time.

Tourist trains began running in 1975, stopping at the pin truss. Passengers could get off, cross Clear Creek on a foot bridge, and enjoy a picnic. When the rail reached all the way down to the abutment for the Devil's Gate Viaduct, a temporary boarding platform was built. A temporary bridge was built over Clear Creek, and wooden stairs, combined with a trail, allowed passengers to reach the platform on the second level of track. A platform was built around the Silver Plume depot making boarding at this end relatively simple and far less physically demanding than boarding at the Georgetown end.

All work on the Georgetown Loop came to a halt in 1977. The State didn't have the money in its budget to continue with the next phase,

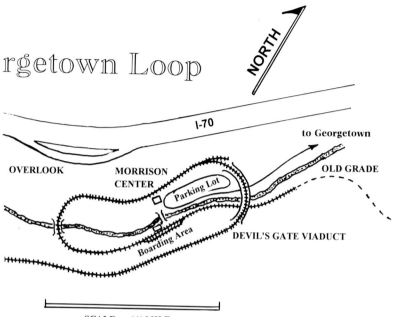

rgetown Loop

NORTH

I-70

OVERLOOK MORRISON CENTER to Georgetown OLD GRADE

Parking Lot

Boarding Area DEVIL'S GATE VIADUCT

SCALE 1/4 MILE

replacement of the high bridge. For five years, the project remained at a stand still with trains running from Silver Plume down to the loading area near the high bridge. John C. Mitchell, president and executive director of the Boettcher Foundation, announced on May 15, 1982, that the organization would make a one million dollar grant to the Georgetown Loop Historic Mining Area to rebuild the high bridge.

The URS Company and Flatiron Structures received the contract for the bridge. Due to modern safety requirements and the increased weight of the locomotives, the bridge had to be redesigned. Every effort, however, was made to make the new bridge look identical to the original bridge. The original bridge sat on stone abutments which were simply laid on the ground. The new bridge required concrete abutments sunk to bedrock. The supporting legs had to be increased from the original eight inches in diameter to twelve or fourteen inches.

During the first year of operation, tourist trains would stop at the pin truss and passengers would be allowed to get off. There was a foot bridge across Clear Creek and a picnic area. It gave the train crew time to relax. (photograph by Kenneth Jessen)

Ground breaking took place on May 2, 1983. The first order of business was to build sixteen reinforced concrete piers to support the bridge. The old granite blocks, which composed the original abutments, had to be removed. New reinforced concrete abutments, many times the size of the original ones, were poured. In August, the steel legs were set, and the eight towers were completed by Labor Day, 1983. The thirty foot cross sections were lowered into place, one by one. Crews lowered the sixty foot center section into place late in September. The final piece of construction came when a professional track laying crew put track across the high bridge, around to a low trestle over Clear Creek, then back to a new loading area. The rails were extended a short distance under the high bridge to complete the spiral. A visitor center, including a theater, was constructed near the lower parking lot above Georgetown, and the old wooden pedestrian bridge across Clear Creek was replaced with a modern concrete bridge.

Track laying reached the Hall Mine overpass by the end of July, 1976. As evidenced by this photograph, track laying was hard work. Not only did rail have to be moved by muscle, the spikes had to be driven by hand using a spike mall. (photograph by Kenneth Jessen)

On June 1, 1984, the first train ventured across the Devil's Gate Viaduct. Two Shay geared locomotives were used to load test the structure. But it wasn't until August 1 that the official grand opening took place, with Governor Richard Lamm as the guest speaker. After a number of speeches, the first official train came down to the upper abutment. Long strings of red, white and blue balloons had been tied at intervals on the rail across the high bridge such that when the locomotive went across, its wheels would cut the strings and the balloons would float aloft. What the organizers failed to count on was that one of the cars, a cattle car carrying members of the press, would derail just short of the bridge. All of the people in that car were standing on one side. This, combined with uneven track, contributed to the derailment. Governor Lamm and his wife rode in the locomotive and were unaffected by this momentary break in the action. The three cars ahead of the cattle car were uncoupled and pulled across the bridge leaving the rest of the train behind. Other trips, free to the public, followed throughout the day.

This August 1977 photograph shows the author's son, Todd, standing in front of the staircase leading to the upper level of track and a temporary boarding platform. A detached piece of track sits on the ground to remind visitors of future plans to complete the loop. (photograph by Kenneth Jessen)

The Georgetown Loop operates during the summer season, and as part of the ticket, a tour of the Lebanon mine can be purchased. The trip over the loop can be made in open cars or enclosed cars and is quite spectacular, especially crossing the Devil's Gate Viaduct. Since there is no means of turning the locomotive at either end of the line, the locomotive operates backward going downgrade and faces forward for the upgrade portion of the trip. At either end, a passing track is used to run the locomotive around the train so that it is always positioned in the front of the train.

This is how the original Devil's Gate Viaduct looked with an excursion train. It was completed in January, 1884. (Colorado Historical Society F32557)

By October, 1983, the center span on the new Devil's Gate Viaduct was in place and the bridge was ready for its decking. (photograph by Kenneth Jessen)

Governor Lamm addresses the crowd on the opening day of the Georgetown Loop, August 1, 1984. (photograph by Kenneth Jessen)

This was the first official train crossing the Devil's Gate Viaduct. As the wheels of the engine passed over the rail, they cut strings holding long streamers of red, white and blue balloons. (photograph by Kenneth Jessen)

Crossing the Devil's Gate Viaduct is always a thrill. The locomotive runs backwards on the trip down, and at the loading area on the Georgetown end, a siding allows the locomotive to run around to the front of the train for the trip back up grade. (photograph by Kenneth Jessen)

This train has just backed down under the Devil's Gate Viaduct after taking on passengers at the Morrison Center on the Georgetown end of the line. Powered by Shay #12, it will now head up the track, over the Devil's Gate Viaduct, around the two loops and on to Silver Plume. (photograph by Kenneth Jessen)

HISTORIC GEORGETOWN PRESERVES HISTORY

After the silver boom of the late 1800s and after a brief resurgence in mining activity during the twentieth century, Georgetown slumbered in a partially abandoned state. Its heritage included many beautiful homes and commercial buildings along with a number of mines and mining structures. In 1966, the National Park Service and the Colorado Historical Society took and inventory of what remained and designated the Georgetown-Silver Plume area as a National Historic Landmark District. The district boundaries are quite large and include the two towns, the entire valley including the railroad grade, as well as many of the mines high on the sides of Republican, Griffith and Leavenworth mountains. Also important was the inclusion of the entire railroad grade of the Georgetown Loop between Silver Plume and Georgetown.

In 1970, Historic Georgetown, Inc. (formerly The Georgetown Society) was founded by four local citizens; Robert Gibbs, Ron Neely, Robert Bolander (deceased) and Wally Baehler (deceased). Their mission focused on the preservation of the district and the restoration of residential buildings within Georgetown.

The Hamill House had undergone many uses since the Hamill family left Georgetown in 1914, including a boarding house and, in 1954, a museum. Historic Georgetown decided to purchase the structure in 1971 and restore the building and its interior to its Victorian elegance. The purchase put the organization into a $100,000 debt in the form of a twenty year mortgage. The mortgage, by the way, was paid off five years early. Over the years, however, an additional half a million dollars has been invested in the Hamill House's restoration with another quarter of a million scheduled in the near future.

When the Hamill House was acquired, it contained few original furnishings, but the walnut woodwork, downstairs wall and ceiling papers and four fireplace mantles were still in place. Progress on restoration was set back by a 1974 fire which damaged the rear gable portion of the house. After reconstruction of the fire damaged area, restoration continued.

The work requires a great deal of research into how the house once looked and was furnished. Historic Georgetown was placed in the

91

position of trying to find furniture similar to that which was once owned by the Hamill family. It is important to note that the Hamill House is recorded in the Smithsonian Institution's collection of American decorative arts at the Cooper-Hewitt Museum in New York City.

In 1974, Historic Georgetown purchased the Bowman-White House to represent the middle class. Plans call for its restoration and opening to the public as a museum. A small cabin, located in the path of I-70, was saved from destruction and moved to property owned by Historic Georgetown behind the Bowman-White House. Its origin and date of construction is unknown, but it represents the more primitive log structures which once dotted the valley. To illustrate that not all Georgetown residents lived in large, expensive homes, the small Tucker-Rutherford House was moved in 1976-1977 to its present location on 9th Street after having been donated to Historic Georgetown. Plans call for its restoration as well.

Historic Georgetown also owns 500 acres of open space in addition to the land occupied by the Hamill House, the Bowman-White House, the old cabin and the Tucker-Rutherford House. It also owns the Henry Kneisel Anderson Park at Biddle and Main.

There is a selection of five categories of membership for Historic Georgetown. The organization has a monthly mailing alternating between a newsletter, a bulletin and a journal. They also sponsor two or three fund raising events a year as well as a lecture series, walking tours and other cultural events.

Although Historic Georgetown is the largest non-profit organization in town, there are three others: The Colonial Dames that operate the Hotel de Paris as a museum, the Georgetown Community Center Ltd. that owns the old county courthouse and operates it as the Community Center, and the Georgetown Energy Museum Foundation concentrating on the preservation of the old hydroelectric plant at the end of 6th Street. Membership in these organizations totals well over a thousand individuals. The Colorado Historical Society manages the Georgetown Loop Historic Mining and Railroad Park.

Could Georgetown become to the history of mining in the American West what Colonial Williamsburg is to the preservation of colonial life in Virginia?

BIBLIOGRAPHY

Booklets

Bradley, Christine. *William A. Hamill.* Fort Collins: Colorado State University, 1977.

Chandler, Polly. *This is Georgetown.* self-published, 1972.

Draper, Benjamin Poff. *Georgetown.* self-published, 1940.

Georgetown Silver Plume - Guide to the Historic District. Evergreen: Cordillera Press, 1990.

Hotel de Paris and Louis Dupuy. Denver: The State Historical Society of Colorado et. al.

Leyendecker, Liston E. *Georgetown, Colorado's Silver Queen.* 1859-1976. Fort Collins: Centennial Publications, 1977.

Morgan, Gary. *Rails Around the Loop.* Fort Collins: Centennial Publications, 1976

The Georgetown Loop. Denver: The Colorado Historical Society, 1986.

The Story of a Valley. Denver: The State Historical Society of Colorado, 1984.

Books

Cook, John W. *Hands Up.* Denver: W. F. Robinson Printing, 1897, pp. 315-322.

Dallas, Sandra. *Gaslight and Gingerbread.* Denver: Sage Books, 1965, pp. 126-131.

Digerness, David S. *The Mineral Belt* Vol. I. Denver: Sundance Publications, 1977, pp. 23-33.

Digerness, David S. *The Mineral Belt* Vol. II. Denver: Sundance Publications, 1982, pp. 15-171.

Dorset, Phyllis Flanders. *The New Eldorado.* New York: The MacMillan Company, 1970, pp. 195-208

Fossett, Frank. *Colorado its Gold and Silver Mines.* New York: C. G. Crawford, 1879, pp. 355-403.

Griswold, P. R., Richard Kindig, Cynthia Trombly. *Georgetown and the Loop.* Denver: Rocky Mountain Railroad Club, 1988.

Hafen, LeRoy R. ed. *Colorado and Its People.* New York: Lewis Historical Publications, 1948, pp. 258-261.

Hauck, Cornelius. *Narrow Gauge to Central and Silver Plume.* Golden: The Colorado Railroad Museum, 1972, pp. 73-189.

History of Clear Creek County. Idaho Springs: Historical Society of Idaho Springs, 1986, pp. 23-27, 189, 196-197, 202.

Horner, John Willard. *Silver Town.* Caldwell, Idaho: Caxton Printers, 1950.

Leyendecker, Liston E. *The Pelican-Dives Feud.* Denver: The State Historical Society, 1985, pp. 39-59.

The Georgetown Loop. Denver: Colorado Historical Society, 1986

Wolle, Muriel Sibell. *Stampede to Timberline.* Denver: Sage Books, 1949, pp. 114-122.

Articles

Bradley, Christine. "Early Days of Georgetown's Volunteer Fire Department." *The Georgetown/Silver Plume National Historic Landmark District Journal,* Vol. 1, No. 1.

DePew, Kathryn. "William A. Hamill." *The Colorado Magazine,* Vol.. XXXII, No. 4 (October, 1955), pp. 266-279.

Digerness, Helen Sidney. "Jesse Summers Randall and Pioneer Georgetown." *The Colorado Magazine,* Vol. XXII, No. 6 (November, 1945), pp. 258-265.

Evans, John "President's Annual Address." *The Colorado Magazine,* Vol. XXV, No. 1, pp. 8-9

Gressley, Gene M. "Hotel de Paris and its Creator." *The Colorado Magazine,* Vol. XXXII, No. 1 (June, 1955), pp. 28-42.

"Interesting bits of History." *The Colorado Magazine*, Vol. XXII, No. 4 (July, 1945), pp. 187-188.

Leyendecker, Liston. "The Lebanon Mill and Mine Complex." *The Colorado Magazine,* Vol. 55, Nos. 2/3 (Spring/Summer, 1978), pp. 161-180.

Russell, James E. "Louis Dupuy and the Hotel de Paris of Georgetown." *The Colorado Magazine,* Vol. XIII, No. 6 (November, 1936), pp. 210-215.

Spence, Clark C. "Colorado's Terrible Mine: A Study in British Investment." *The Colorado Magazine*, Vol. XXXIV, No. 1 (June, 1957), pp. 48-61.

Spring, Agnes Wright. "Theodore Roosevelt in Colorado." The Colorado Magazine, Vol. XXXV, No. 4 (October, 1958), p. 247.

"The Pioneer Bar of Colorado." *The Colorado Magazine*, Vol. I, No. 5 (July, 1925), p. 200.

Newspaper Articles

"A Double Life." *The Georgetown Courier,* June 6, 1888.

"A Man is Lynched Here!" *Denver Field and Farming*, March 12, 1898.

"Our Town is Nicknamed Silver Queen." *The Colorado Miner,* June 6, 1872.

The Story of Edward Bainbridge - see *The Central City Register,* April 23 and April 26, 1867

"Georgetown - The Christening." *The Georgetown Courier,* December 25, 1920.

Index